STRATEGIC MANAGEMENT IN THE UNITED STATES AND JAPAN

STRATEGIC MANAGEMENT IN THE UNITED STATES AND JAPAN
A Comparative Analysis

Edited by
ROSALIE L. TUNG

BALLINGER PUBLISHING COMPANY
Cambridge, Massachusetts
A Subsidiary of Harper & Row, Publishers, Inc.

Copyright © 1986 by Ballinger Publishing Company, with the exception of Chapter 6—Strategic Issues for the General Trading Companies, copyright © by Thomas B. Lifson. All rights reserved. No part of this publication may be reproduced, stored in a retrieval system, or transmitted in any form or by any means, electronic, mechanical, photocopy, recording or otherwise, without the prior written consent of the publisher.

International Standard Book Number: 0-88730-089-8

Library of Congress Catalog Card Number: 86-1169

Printed in the United States of America

Library of Congress Cataloging-in-Publication Data

Strategic management in the United States and Japan.

"Articles . . . based on papers presented at a conference held at the Wharton School University of Pennsylvania, in Fall 1984"—Introd.
Includes index.
1. Strategic planning—United States—Congresses.
2. Strategic planning—Japan—Congresses. I. Tung, Rosalie L. (Rosalie Lam), 1948–
HD30.28.S7324 1986   658.4'012'0952   86-1169
ISBN 0-88730-089-8

To Vance F. Mitchell,
my mentor and friend

CONTENTS

List of Figures — xi

List of Tables — xiii

List of Abbreviations and Acronyms — xv

Introduction
—*Rosalie L. Tung* — xvii

PART I   GOVERNMENT-ENTERPRISE INTERFACE

Chapter 1
Japan: The Government-Business Relationship
—*Robert J. Ballon* — 3

Chapter 2
Government-Business Relationships in the United States and Japan: A Comparative Analysis
—*Mitsuaki Sato* — 15

Chapter 3
Comparative Aspects of the Government-Enterprise Interface in the United States and Japan
—*Howard F. Van Zandt* — 23

PART II STRATEGIC ISSUES FOR GENERAL TRADING COMPANIES

Chapter 4
The Uncertain Future of Japan's General Trading Companies
—Stefan H. Robock and Kichiro Hayashi 33

Chapter 5
Strategic Issues for the *Sogo Shosha*
—Hiroshi Kohiyama 47

Chapter 6
Strategic Issues for the General Trading Companies
—Thomas B. Lifson 55

Chapter 7
U.S. Trading Companies: Corporate Organization for Countertrade
—Thaddeus Kopinski 65

PART III STRATEGIC MANAGEMENT IN THE MANUFACTURING SECTOR

Chapter 8
Strategic Management in Manufacturing: The Case of Aircrafts
—Thomas J. Bacher 87

Chapter 9
Strategic Management in Manufacturing: The Case of Pharmaceuticals
—Leonard Wimpfheimer 99

Chapter 10
Management Practices and Business Strategy in Manufacturing Firms
—Vladimir Pucik 115

PART IV   *STRATEGIC MANAGEMENT IN THE FINANCIAL SECTOR*

Chapter 11
A Comparative Analysis of Corporate Capital Structure in the United States and Japan
— *William H. Davidson*   133

Chapter 12
Japanese Corporate Finance and Corporate Capital Structure
— *Takuro Isoda*   151

Index   167

About the Contributors   173

About the Editor   179

LIST OF FIGURES

6-1	Some Types of Actors in the Cotton Textile Product System in Japan	57
6-2	Some Types of Actors in the Japanese Petroleum Product System	60
6-3	The Service Life Cycle	61
8-1	Japan's Targeted Industry Strategy	92
8-2	Japanese Requirements for Success versus Commercial Aircraft Industry Characteristics	93
8-3	How the Aircraft Industry Differs from Other Targeted Industries	95
8-4	Percentage of Sales from the Japanese Domestic Market, High-Export Products	96
9-1	Leading Corporations, World Market, 1983	105
9-2	Japanese Pharmaceutical Market—Market Share versus Number of *Propa*, 1983	106
12-1	Comparison of Interest Rate (payment) and Return on Assets	152
12-2	Relationship between Recurring Profit/Equity and Stockholders' Equity Ratio (manufacturers)	161
12-3	Increase of Real Retained Earnings: All Industries, Capital Stock More Than 1 Billion Yen	163

LIST OF TABLES

1-1	Public Employees per Thousand Population, International Comparison	8
1-2	Employment in the Public Sector, 1980	9
5-1	Mitsubishi's Trading Transaction in Manufactured Goods, March 1985	51
9-1	Major Foreign Corporations in the Japanese Market (ethical pharmaceuticals), 1983	108
11-1	Source of Funds for U.S. and Japanese Manufacturing Corporations	135
11-2	Comparative Financial Ratios for U.S. and Japanese Firms in Seven Manufacturing Industries, 1981	136
11-3	Ratio of Debt to Equity (%) for 256 U.S. and Japanese Manufacturing Corporations	141
11-4	Inflow and Outflow of Funds: April-May 1984	146
12-1	Ways of Financing: Large Companies	154
12-2	Diversification of External Financing in Large Japanese Corporations, All Industries	156
12-3	Questionnaire Survey on Motives for Issuing Bonds in Foreign Currencies	157

12-4	Companywide Breakdown of Borrowings by National Banks (percentage increase versus year earlier)	158
12-5	Change of Equity Ratio: Large Companies	160
12-6	Uses of Funds in Large Companies, All Industries (breakdown: %)	164

LIST OF ABBREVIATIONS AND ACRONYMS

CD	certificate of deposit
CEO	chief executive officer
CTDC	Civil Transport Development Corporation
FDA	Food and Drug Administration
FTC	Federal Trade Commission
GATT	General Agreement on Tariffs and Trade
GTC	general trading company
IMF	International Monetary Fund
IRB	industrial revenue bond
JADC	Japan Aircraft Development Corporation
JETRO	Japan External Trade Organization
JNR	Japan National Railway
LDC	less developed countries
MITI	Ministry of International Trade and Industry
MNC	multinational corporation
MSD	Merck Sharp and Dohme
NHI	National Health Scheme
NTT	Nippon Telegraph and Telephone
OECD	Organization for Economic Cooperation and Development
OEM	Original Equipment Manufacturer
PP&E	property, plant, and equipment
R&D	research and development

INTRODUCTION
Rosalie L. Tung

Over the past several years the attitude of U.S. practitioners and scholars toward Japanese management practices has oscillated from adulation to questioning of their alleged virtues. In the late 1970s and early 1980s scholars exhorted the merits of Japanese management principles. This culminated in the publication of numerous management texts, including two that made their way to the best seller list in the *New York Times*, namely, Ouchi's *Theory Z* (1981) and Pascale and Athos' *The Art of Japanese Management* (1981). There was even a frantic rush to translate Japanese works that purportedly provide insight into the art and secrets of Japanese management, such as Miyamoto Musashi's *The Book of the Five Rings*, which was dubbed as "Japan's response to Harvard's MBA."

Many U.S. firms began to experiment with so-called Japanese management principles. However, in their rush to boost sagging sales and eroding international competitiveness, they often failed to take into full consideration the differences in environmental conditions that prevail in the two countries. Given the environmental variations between the United States and Japan, it is little wonder that such efforts often failed to bear fruit, much less serve as a panacea to the problems that may have plagued their firms. This led to a growing disillusionment and disenchantment with what Japanese management principles can supposedly deliver, as witnessed by the publication of books such as Sethi, Namiki, and Swanson's *The False Prom-*

ise of the Japanese Miracle (1984). U.S. industry, once again, turned inward and tried to find solutions to their problems from fellow U.S. firms. This has accounted in part for the appeal and popularity of Peters and Waterman's *In Search of Excellence: Lessons from America's Best-Run Companies* (1982).

This reversal in attitude toward Japanese management practices may also be viewed as part of a natural evolution inherent to most processes of maturation: In the first phase there is an unquestioning acceptance of the premises. In the second phase the assumptions raised in the earlier period are challenged. The third phase is typically characterized by a period of introspection wherein one begins to have a better understanding of the totality and is thus capable of separating the wheat from the chaff. In terms of the evolutionary phases in our understanding of Japanese management practices, I believe that we have progressed beyond the first two stages and are now on the threshold of the third phase.

This edited book of readings represents an effort in this direction. The articles included in the book are based on papers presented at a conference held at The Wharton School, University of Pennsylvania, in fall 1984. The conference was funded by two of the research centers at Wharton, namely the U.S.-Japan Management Studies Center and the Center for International Management Studies. The theme of the conference was comparative strategic management practices and issues in the United States and Japan. Specifically, it examined the strategic issues in managing the interface between government and enterprise, and strategic management practices in various sectors of the economy, including manufacturing, trading, and finance. The book is divided into parts, each dealing with one of these topics. The contributors include practitioners and academicians from both the United States and Japan. The decision to include both practitioners and academicians stemmed from the recognition that neither group alone could adequately address the issues from both the theoretical and the practical standpoint.

It is interesting to note that although the authors were given considerable leeway to address the issue of comparative strategic management practices in the two countries, many of them arrived at the general conclusion that the strategies indigenous to the United States and Japan were developed in response to the environmental constraints and challenges inherent in the respective countries. Hence, certain policies and strategies may not be directly transferable. At the same time, however, there are important lessons that each can learn from the other in this day of increasing global competition and cooperation. Although the authors are generally agreed on this issue, there is diversity in their interpretation of the present situation and their projections for the future. Given this diversity, it may be neither possible nor desirable to integrate the perspectives presented by the various authors. Rather, the analysis of each author should be allowed to stand on its own to allow readers to draw their own conclusions.

Part I deals with strategic issues in the management of the government-enterprise interface in the United States and Japan. The first piece in the section is by Professor Robert Ballon of Sophia University (Japan). As a resident and scholar of Japanese industrial practices for the past thirty years, Professor Ballon is uniquely qualified to address the subject. Professor Ballon ascribes many of the misconceptions and misunderstandings by the West of Japanese government-enterprise relationships to semantic differences. He alludes to the general problems of trying to view and explain phenomena in other countries through one's own lenses. He specifically cites how the notions of "nation," "government," "private" versus "public," "rights," and "bureaucracy" are essentially Western concepts. Hence, "Western concepts stand for Western experiences," which may account for the commonly held suspicion in the West that the Japanese government and industry conspire to keep out *gaijins* or foreigners. In a similar vein, the second paper in the section, Chapter 2, by Mitsuaki Sato (Director of Japan Trade Center, an overseas arm of the Ministry of International Trade and Industry) tries to correct the widely held misconceptions about Japanese industrial policy. Mr. Sato provides a clear explanation of the concept and points to the problem inherent in many studies comparing the government-enterprise interface in the United States and Japan; namely, the "failure to view the goals and records of the two countries in the context of their respective histories and geographies." He goes on to argue that Japan's industrial policy was developed in response to the combination of societal, cultural, natural, and historical forces unique to the country. Thus, in his opinion, any attempt by the United States to develop an industrial policy along the Japanese model would be inappropriate and hence doomed to failure.

Chapter 3—by Professor Howard Van Zandt of the University of Texas at Dallas, an American who has lived and worked in Japan for twenty-seven years — is a marked departure from Professor Ballon's contention that the Japanese market is presently as open as that of any advanced industrialized nation. Professor Van Zandt takes the position that nontariff barriers to trade still exist and, more importantly, explains why they continue to persist. He then paints a scenario of political strife in the United States which, according to his projections, would be brought on by the population explosion in Mexico. He then discusses their implications for Japan. In his chapter Professor Van Zandt enters into a discussion of the differences in staffing policies between U.S. and Japanese multinationals. He contends that the reason U.S. multinationals, unlike their Japanese counterparts, use host country nationals more extensively in their foreign operations stems from their lack of group consciousness. There are other factors — such as restrictions imposed by host governments on the employment of foreign nationals, high costs, problems of maladjustment, the desire to build better relations with the host country, and to make deeper inroads into the local markets — that are equally if not more important than the issue of group consciousness in the employment of local nationals. Incidentally, Japanese multinationals increasingly recognize the need to localize, that is, to use host country nationals. This is one of the critical issues confronting the future operations of the *sogo shosha*, as addressed in both Chapters 4 and 5.

Part II is devoted to the subject of strategic issues for general trading companies. There are four chapters in this section. The first, Chapter 4, is coauthored by Professors Stefan Robock (Columbia University) and Kichiro Hayashi (Aoyama Gakuin University). The authors begin by explaining the six traditional functions performed by the Japanese general trading company (*sogo shosha*). Based on a comprehensive analysis of the environmental changes, Robock and Hayashi point out that the traditional competitive advantage enjoyed by the *sogo shosha* in each of these functions is eroding rapidly. Consequently, the *sogo shosha* have to develop new strategies to respond to these new environmental forces. However, the authors are quick to point out that they are not writing an obituary for the *sogo shosha*. Rather their purpose is to highlight the need for changes in strategies traditionally espoused by the Japanese general trading companies. Their chapter alludes to many of these evolving strategies. These are further expounded upon by Mr. Hiroshi Kohiyama, then executive vice-president of Mitsubishi International Corporation

(New York) and now director of Mitsubishi Corporation (Japan). Mr. Kohiyama describes three new strategies that have been developed by his company in response to these environmental changes. These include the *shosha*'s more active involvement in foreign direct investment, their engaging in countertrade arrangements, and the provision of a more "comprehensive and flexible array of services" to mature industries that are undergoing transition. The implementation of these new strategies requires a fundamental restructuring of existing organizational structures and changes in personnel policies, primarily in terms of hiring host country nationals. In Chapter 6 Dr. Thomas Lifson of Harvard University further elaborates on the role of the *sogo shosha* as "product systems." Although much has been said and written about the *sogo shosha*, the intricacies of their operations remain an enigma to many in the United States because there is no equivalent organizational system in this country. Consequently, Dr. Lifson's piece provides valuable insight into their operations. It is ironic to note that at a time when the Japanese general trading companies are undergoing a crisis situation, the United States should, by and large, view the establishment of general trading companies (as witnessed by the passage of the Export Trading Act in October 1982) as a way to redress the problem of large balance-of-trade deficits and thus regain its global competitive edge. Chapter 7 by Mr. Thaddeus Kopinski, senior editor of Business International, focuses on corporate organizational forms for undertaking countertrade obligations. A cursory review of the statistics on countertrade highlights the need for U.S. multinationals to understand this emerging trend in international trade. Some experts have estimated countertrade to account for as much as 20 percent of total world trade; the General Agreement on Tariffs and Trade (GATT) has suggested a lower figure of 5 percent or approximately $40 billion per annum. Some eighty-eight countries in the world now require some form of countertrade as a precondition for economic cooperation with firms from other countries. Because of this new economic reality, Mr. Kopinski points to the need for U.S. multinationals to engage in countertrade. It should be recalled that countertrade was also cited by Mr. Kohiyama as one of the three new strategies adopted by Mitsubishi. To cope with this situation, multinationals have to develop new organizational forms or structures to accommodate these activities. In his chapter Mr. Kopinski identifies five mechanisms for handling countertrade activities. He then alludes to the important considerations in establishing a trading subsidiary. Mr. Kopinski examines the question of whether a trading subsidiary should be allowed to work for third parties. It is interesting that this issue should be raised because a general trading company, by nature and definition, should be allowed to handle the products of other companies; otherwise, they are little different from the international or export division of the company. This issue perhaps illustrates the spirit of individualism characteristic in the United States and may explain in part why U.S. export trading companies have not fared well thus far. An estimated forty export trading companies have been formed in the United States since the passage of the Export Trading Act in late 1982. Only General Electric Trading Corporation is expected to break even by yearend 1985 (*Wall Street Journal* 1984). In the case of General Electric Trading Corporation, for example, it is estimated that 90 percent of the company's exports are General Electric's own products. As indicated in Kopinski's chapter, more profits could be generated if the trading unit were allowed to handle third-party products.

Part III deals with strategic management in the manufacturing sector. The first chapter is by Mr. Thomas Bacher, director of International Business, Boeing Commercial Airplane Company. His chapter deals with the subject of economic collaboration between Boeing and Civil Transport Development Corporation (CTDC) in the aerospace industry, a sector targeted for growth by the Japanese government in the 1980s. Because of the special characteristics associated with the aerospace industry, Mr. Bacher contends that developments in this field will not resemble those of the automobile sector. This is, of course, a debatable issue. He further hypothesizes that because of the highly positive experiences encountered by Boeing in their cooperative agreements with the Japanese thus far, the Boeing–CTDC venture may establish a model of collaboration between U.S. and Japanese firms in other industries, such as genetic engineering and computers. Similarly, Chapter 9 — by Mr. Leonard Wimpfheimer, director of Japan Operations, Merck Sharp & Dohme International, a subsidiary of Merck & Company — contends that the Japanese should not have a comparative advantage over the Americans and Europeans in the pharmaceutical industry. Besides comparing the strategies pursued by U.S. and Japanese pharmaceutical firms to date, Mr. Wimpfheimer identifies five strategies that foreign companies can adopt when entering Japan, the second-largest pharmaceutical market in the free world. He then discusses the pros and cons associated with each of these five strategies for penetrating the Japanese market: licensing, joint venturing, direct distribution with an independent sales force, codevelopment and comarketing of a specific product, and acquisition of a majority equity position in an established Japanese company. Based upon this analysis, he came to the conclusion that the appropriate strategy for marketing pharmaceuticals in Japan depends largely on the corporate objectives of the specific company. Chapter 10 is by Dr. Vladimir Pucik of the University of Michigan. Dr. Pucik illustrates how the so-called competitive strategies of Japanese manufacturing companies are influenced by internal management practices, such as the emphasis on increasing market share over the goal of short-term profitability, the labor market situation, and intense intercompany competition. Based on his analysis, he discusses their implications for U.S. firms, particularly in terms of cooperative ventures with Japanese partners. Using examples, he illustrates why certain cooperative ventures work while others do not. He concludes by identifying some of the important considerations in the establishment of such cooperative agreements.

The final section in the book, Part IV, examines the subject of strategic management in the financial sector. Two pieces are included in this section. The first is by Dr. William Davidson, now with the University of Southern California, who provides a comparative analysis of the financial structure, philosophy, and performance of U.S. and Japanese firms. His analysis is based on empirical data collected from 266 major U.S. and Japanese companies. Based on his comprehensive survey of the historical data, Dr. Davidson arrives at the conclusion that the competitive advantage of the Japanese can be attributed mainly to the structure of Japanese financial markets and corporate finance. This is, of course, only one of the numerous hypotheses that have been advanced to date to account for Japan's "economic miracle." Other theses include the existence of an industrial policy and the efficient allocation and utilization of human resources. If Dr. Davidson's contention that Japan's "ability to operate with lower margins and returns" constitutes its principal competitive advantage in the global arena were true, the basis for this advantage may be fast eroding because, according to Chapter 12—by Mr. Takuro Isoda, president of Daiwa Securities (America) Inc.—the Japanese financial market and corporate financial structure will more closely resemble that of the United States. According to Mr. Isoda's projection, in the not too distant future, financial profit will play a role, equal in importance to operating profit, in Japanese corporate financial management. Besides this projection of the future evolution of Japanese corporate financial structure, Mr. Isoda also provides a good summary of the changes in corporate financial practices in Japan over time and discusses their implications for management.

The twelve chapters included in this book provide valuable insights into numerous aspects of comparative strategic management in different industrial sectors in the United States and Japan. Three general insights can be surmised from the collection. One, strategies are developed in the context of the peculiar environmental constraints and challenges confronting a given country and industry. Consequently, what is appropriate for a given country or industry may not necessarily apply in another. Two, although the authors do not provide solutions to all the strategic issues that may arise in the respective industrial sectors in the 1980s and beyond, they do shed light on what some of the more successful companies are doing in this regard. Three, in light of the increasing globalization of industries, the competitive strategy for the 1980s and beyond call for firms from both the United States and Japan (and other countries, of course) to enter into more collaborative agreements that can take full advantage of the opportunities and challenges that lie ahead, and thus generate synergy. To make these global cooperative ventures work, each side needs to have a better understanding of the other's perspective, particularly in the context of how strategic management issues are handled. As illustrated in the various chapters of the book, many of these cooperative agreements can work, such as that between Boeing and CTDC, Merck Sharp & Dohme and Banyu, and Mitsubishi and its North American allies. These cases show that although there are problems to collaboration that may stem in part from the dissimiliarities in the management of strategic issues, these barriers can be surmounted and both sides can gain from the cooperative efforts.

REFERENCES

Musashi, Miyamato. 1982. *The Book of Five Rings*. Translated by Nihon Services Corporation. New York: Bantam Books.
Ouchi, William G. 1981. *Theory Z*. Reading, Mass.: Addison-Wesley.

Peters, Thomas J., and Robert H. Waterman, Jr. 1982. *In Search of Excellence: Lessons from America's Best-Run Companies.* New York: Warner Books Inc.

Pascale, Richard T., and Anthony G. Athos. 1981. *The Art of Japanese Management.* New York: Simon and Schuster.

Sethi, S. Prakash; Nobuki Namiki; and Carl L. Swanson. 1984. *The False Promise of the Japanese Miracle.* Marshfield, Mass.: Pitman Publishing Inc.

Wall Street Journal. 1984. May 24: 1.

I GOVERNMENT-ENTERPRISE INTERFACE

1 JAPAN
The Government-Business Relationship

Robert J. Ballon

The task of discussing various aspects of the government-business relationship in Japan is frustrating for two main reasons. One, so many of the terms we use are tradition bound on both sides of the Pacific, but by a different tradition. To reconcile differences in semantics by the mere use of the dictionary is not adequate: The words may have been translated, but not necessarily their meaning. Two, precisely this effort at catching meanings in their original context is frustrating, because tradition-bound terms are also value laden. Their meaning may well come to depend on one's individual view on the current, or previous, style of national administration.

SEMANTICS

Many of the misconceptions about the government-business relationship in Japan stem from semantics. In general, Western concepts stand for Western experiences. Hence, many of the terms and concepts used to characterize events and happenings in the Western world may be inappropriate for describing non-Western, Japanese experiences. Terms such as "nation," "government," "private" versus "public," and "rights" suffer from fundamentally different meanings in the contexts of Western and Japanese experiences. Some of these differences are examined below.

Nation

To state that Japan is the nation of the Japanese calls on the Western and relatively recent experience of "nation." Historians are generally in agreement that the concept of nationalism has its roots in Europe and can be traced to the Peace of Westphalia in 1648. By 1648 Japan was already a centuries-old reality. Thus, the Western concept of "nation" does not quite apply in the Japanese setting.

Government

After two unsuccessful attempts by the Mongols to conquer Japan—one in 1274 and the other in 1281—Japan was able to exist through the centuries without subjugation by external forces. In 1945 Japan was invaded for the first time. In Western experience, the notion of government usually refers to some central authority, most often imposed from above and outside through divine right or conquest. The power of a government is based on fear on its ability to coerce. In Japanese experience, the authority of the government is not so much conferred from outside by law or the political process; rather, it is something that arose from the inner needs of a homogeneous and highly integrated society. Under this different set of circumstances, power is largely based on faith.

Public and Private

The Western concept of private evolved from the experience of individualism and property. It entails rights and independence, which in the West have a positive connotation and become ultimate values. Public, on the other hand, implies dependence, which has a negative connotation. In sharp contrast, the Japanese experience of public implies harmony, mutuality, and unity; it is a positive notion and embodies ultimate values in a collective context. It stands for interdependence. Private, on the other hand, tends to be equated with a negation of this vital interdependence. As yet, however, neither of these terms has acquired the specificity in Japan that they enjoy in the Western context.

Japanese social dynamics operate on the basis of interdependence. Whereas Western interaction tends to be of the type, 1 + 1 = 2, in Japan the formula would be 1 × 1 = 1. Thus, in Japan the reality of government and business is not that of two entities to be somehow added up but rather the reality of one coin with two faces. In other words, two distinct but interdependent institutions, namely the government and business, form one reality: Japan. In Japan the Western notion of laissez faire, which supposes a gap between the public and private sectors, has never made sense. Although for Japanese the private is not the public, the dividing line between the two is not always clear. Furthermore, the private sector is explicitly endowed with expectations and responsibilities that are public in nature, as in the case of national emergencies in Western countries.

Rights

The political system of the Tokugawa era (1600–1868) was inspired by neo-Confucianism as a philosophy of society and hence of the state. In this neo-Confucian order, individualism had no place as a social force; rather, society was looked at as a system of interpersonal relationships along a vertical axis.

After 1868, when Japan was forced to adopt a "modern" legal system (i.e., following the pattern of Western societies), there was no direct translation for the term "right." Everything had always been expressed in terms of "duty," mutual duty. The present-day term, *kenri*, the equivalent of right, was introduced as a translation of the Western term. Despite the adoption of the Western concept of right, the fact remains that the architects of modern Japan were mostly former warrior-bureaucrats who traditionally had formulated, interpreted, and administered the country in a manner consistent with the social system of mutual obligations.

Bureaucracy

In the context of the government-business relationship, "government" stands not so much for the political parties and the cabinet or the chief of state, but for bureaucracy. Each ministry is headed by a minister, who is a member of the cabinet, and at least two vice-ministers, one of whom is a political appointee and the other an administrative vice-minister. In postwar Japan cabinets have had a life of one to two years. However, since 1945, except for an eighteen-month period of coalition cabinets—from May 1947 to October 1948—the majority in the Diet has always been the same, namely conservative. Partially as a result, there has been no reshuffling in the bureaucracy when a new cabinet is installed. Continuity is guaranteed by the administrative vice-minister, who comes up from the ranks of each ministry. Like most of the other higher officials and top management in the private sector, the administrative vice-minister has attended the same schools and sometimes may even possess the common family ties.

Ever since the inception of modern Japan in 1868, the higher echelon of civil service has been a most coveted career which is something to be begun immediately upon graduation from university. Even today the brightest graduates from the elite universities enter the most prestigious ministries, on the basis of rigorous examination and selective recommendation. After early retirement in their fifties they either enter politics, or head public corporations, or join the board of large corporations.

HISTORICAL PERSPECTIVE

The role of the government has changed over the centuries. Under Confucianism the government was viewed as a teacher. This changed during the Meiji Restoration. After World War II and the subsequent national emergencies, the role of the government evolved to meet the changing times.

The Government as Teacher

According to Confucianism, the role of the State is not that of a policeman but rather that of a teacher. The homogeneity and high degree of integration of the Japanese people express themselves spontaneously at a nationwide level, making the government the epitome of national identity.

Throughout its modern history, Japan and Japanese business have been struggling against odds that no individual firm or industry could adequately face: threat of foreign dominance, scarcity of natural resources, pressure of population, and so on. These were all national emergencies. The preoccupation with national survival has been readily expressed in a "competition-against-the-whole-world" syndrome, as exhibited by the militaristic drive until 1945, and by the drive for growth thereafter. The concern for national survival always requires the mobilization of the energies of the entire nation, with contributions from the public and private sectors, under the aegis of the government, or more specifically, of the bureaucracy. The rehabilitation after World War II and the orientation toward growth necessitated the government to play a strong role to steer the country, as a collectivity, on its course.

Meiji Government: Initiator of Industry

What must be appreciated is the fact that industrialization in Japan was not started by private entrepreneurs, but by the government. After 1868 it took the Meiji government almost two decades to finally convince the private sector, traditionally most active in commerce, to join the bandwagon of industrialization. At the first signs of interest, the government turned over to private interests most of its industrial ventures. As with government contracts even today, this process of "denationalization" called for little, if any, competitive bidding. Government enterprises were allocated to whomever was believed to be able to operate them most beneficially and usually most efficiently, to the long-term interest of the nation.

Postwar Government: From Regulator to Partner

In postwar Japan two stages of the government-business relationship can be distinguished. Up to about the mid-1960s regulation prevailed, starting with state trading immediately after the war and ending with the beginnings of liberalization, when Japan joined the Organization for Economic Cooperation and Development (OECD) and the International Monetary Fund (IMF). The second stage was one of steady deregulation, wherein over the course of two decades the Japanese economy became as open as that of any major Western nation.

Table 1-1. Public Employees per Thousand Population, International Comparison.

	Japan (1980)	U.K. (1978)	F.R.G. (1979)	U.S. (1980)
National public employees	7.7	8.7	2.4	8.6
National defense	2.5	9.5	10.7	13.4
Government enterprises	8.1	37.4	14.1	—
Subtotal (A)	18.3	55.6	27.3	22.1
Local public employees (B)	26.6	53.7	48.5	60.4
Total (A + B)	44.9	109.4	75.8	82.4
Total (minus defense)	42.4	99.9	56.0	69.0

Source: Kiyoaki Tsuji, ed., *Public Administration in Japan* (Tokyo: University of Tokyo Press, 1980), pp. 72-73.

The immediate postwar national emergency and reconstruction of the economy could not take place without an all-out orchestration by the bureaucracy, particularly after the attempt by the Allied Occupation authorities to dismantle the prewar industrial establishment or *zaibatsu*.

In the late 1950s a new kind of national emergency developed. This took the form of trade and capital liberalization coupled with balance-of-payment problems. Under these circumstances the bureaucracy had to adopt the following measures:

- protecting agriculture for political reasons;
- protecting small and medium firms, particularly in the distribution sector;
- providing growth-oriented industries with all the domestic market they could get; and
- phasing out declining industries.

In the late 1960s a twin national emergency prevailed: public demands for improvement of the environment and external pressures for so-called internationalization (*kokusai-ka*).

In the 1970s various shocks, such as the Nixon shock and oil shocks, jolted the nation. This brought the period of high growth

Table 1-2. Employment in the Public Sector, 1980.

At the national level		
General ministries and agencies	362,858	
National schools and hospitals	181,432	
Self-defense forces	272,162	
Diet, courts, etc.	30,650	
Five government enterprises		
(PTT and monopolies)	352,541	1,199,643
Public corporations		
Japan National Railway	413,594	
Nippon Telegraph & Telephone	327,171	
Others	189,705	930,470
Local public employees		
Prefectures	1,725,090	
Municipalities and others	1,480,628	3,205,718
Total		5,335,831

Source: Kiyoaki Tsuji, ed., *Public Administration in Japan* (Tokyo: University of Tokyo Press, 1980), pp. 72-73.

to an abrupt end, thus provoking a major restructuring of the industrial setup.

In the early 1980s international trade frictions and U.S. pressure for rearmament are viewed as the immediate national emergencies.

Present-day Small Government

Despite these requirements for public intervention, the Japanese government has remained relatively small. In 1980, out of 50 million people that were engaged in nonagricultural employment, 40 million were salaried workers, out of which 5.3 million were employed in the public sector. See Tables 1-1 and 1-2.

FORMS OF INTERACTION

The interaction between government and business can take one of several forms. These include control, planning, investment spending, the extension of subsidies and low-interest loans, development, protection, and the promotion of imports.

Control

Control, in the sense of allocation of resources and production capacity, was exercised in the early postwar years and extended until the enactment of the 1961 Petroleum Industry Act. At no time, however, was nationalization considered a proper method. By 1985 Nippon Telegraph and Telephone (NTT) has become a private enterprise. At the time of writing, the privatization and reorganization of Japan National Railway (JNR), which was formed through the nationalization program of 1906 which absorbed important private lines, is being prepared.

Planning

Broadly speaking, the national planning process consists of the following activities: One, government agencies interact constantly with industry through hundreds of joint consultation committees (discussed in greater detail later). Two, each agency establishes the specific plans and policies for its own sphere of jurisdiction within the context of the national budget. Three, the Ministry of Finance coordinates all these plans in preparation of the national budget. Four, the Economic Planning Agency, which can be compared to a corporate planning department, acts as an advisory agency to the cabinet, defining the general direction to be pursued by the economy. The Economic Planning Agency thus also exerts some influence in the coordination of public expenditures.

Investment Spending

About one-third of all investments are made by the government through economic development projects, which usually take the form of public works. They are funded out of tax revenue (which make up about two-thirds of the investment spending), special accounts (i.e., private savings, such as postal, annuities, and insurances), and beginning in the 1970s, government bonds.

Often, the government establishes the basic funding of what eventually becomes an independent private entity. Many of the research and training institutes were established along these lines.

Subsidies and Low-cost Lending

In the immediate postwar reconstruction period there was considerable extension of outright subsidies to industry. Today, direct subsidies are seldom used, except in the agricultural sector, where political realities dictate public policy.

After the immediate postwar reconstruction era the extension of direct subsidies was replaced largely by low-cost government loans. A beneficiary of this program was the automobile industry in the 1950s. In the period of rapid growth right up to the early 1970s, under the principle of administrative guidance by the Ministry of Finance, cash flowed from the low-growth to high-growth industries, using the debt capacity of established firms, say from textiles to steel and chemicals. Commercial banks were the principal vehicle for such flows, with government banks acting as "pump primers." Today, such lending is effective in progressively phasing out declining industries, such as aluminum. Throughout the postwar period small to medium enterprises remained the primary beneficiaries of such low-cost financing programs, primarily through the formation of special financial institutions.

Development

During the 1950s, 1960s, and early 1970s the government actively promoted the development of new industries through regulating the introduction of new technology. The most famous case is that of the computer industry in the 1960s, where the Ministry of International Trade and Industry (MITI) took a strong initiative in limiting imports, sponsoring technology development, financing rentals to end-users, and directly influencing the strategies of the major competitors. The government is not always successful with such plans, however, as was the case with the automobile industry. Today, such developments take the form of so-called national projects. These national projects include nuclear energy, space development, ocean exploration, computers, and environmental protection and safety.

Protection

Unlike Western practices of protectionism, the Japanese government has traditionally protected growth industries rather than declining ones. In the early postwar period the primary legal instrument was foreign exchange controls. In addition, the 1952 Export-Import Law permitted a given industry, with the concurrence of MITI and the Federal Trade Commission (FTC), to establish a temporary export cartel to control price and quantity of designated products to specific markets. This was referred to as the system of orderly marketing. The administration of voluntary quotas, for all practical purposes, requires some form of cartel.

After the mid-1960s, with successive rounds of trade and capital liberalization, Japan has become as open as major Western countries. Measures other than protection are now employed to promote industrial structural change. Thus, the Japanese trade surplus results mainly from successful exports rather than restrictions on imports.

Promotion of Imports

In fact, since the mid-1970s and in an increasing number of ways, imports into Japan are officially promoted. This task is entrusted among others to the Japan External Trade Organization (JETRO), an agency under the jurisdiction of MITI. In mid-1985, for example, an elaborate "market-opening action program" was adopted by the Japanese government.

MAIN INSTRUMENTS FOR INTERACTION

The aforementioned forms of interaction between government and business were carried out through one or more of three primary forms: administrative guidance, consensus, and industrial policy.

Administrative Guidance

Administrative guidance is best understood in the tradition of the pre-Meiji era—the warrior-bureaucrat made, interpreted, and administered the "law" as a rule of equity. It was not, but did not necessarily exclude, arbitrariness on the part of bureaucracy. This function resulted basically from the role of the government as teacher and the need for consensus to be implemented. The penalty for not accepting administrative guidance was not direct, but indirect, discontinuity of interaction.

Even in the early postwar years, the practical purpose of administrative guidance was never to introduce nationalization. On the contrary, it was aimed at helping and encouraging private initiative. At times, though, this attitude may have been ill advised, but it remained well intentioned.

The fact that a number of senior-ranking government officials join private industry upon retirement, primarily those sectors over which they had administered, helps the process substantially. Thus, former officials of the Ministry of Finance join financial institutions; those from MITI join manufacturing companies; those from the Ministry of Health and Welfare join pharmaceutical companies, and so on.

The ultimate function of administrative guidance is consensus building.

Consensus

Consensus takes one or more of the following forms: One, consensus is a technique for resolving problems. This does not mean an inherent unity of policy. Rather, it provides a unique context for resolving conflict. It should be noted that neither the various government agencies nor the industries nor the members of an industry speak with one voice.

Two, consensus is carried out in specific terms. It should not be construed as a technique of planning, except at best in the sense of an implicit agreement on guidelines at a given time. On broad issues, interaction takes place mostly between the cabinet and/or ministries and the Federation of Economic Associations (*Keidanren*). Particular issues, however, are handled between the specific industry and its respective ministry or bureau.

Three, consensus building requires flexibility on the parts of both government and business. The bureaucracy almost always drafts the bills after extensive consultation with the private sector, the Diet then legislates a broad charter law, and the bureaucracy ultimately interprets and administers the law. Thus, broad priorities are established at the cabinet level, while expenditure and revenue allocation are delegated to the bureaucracy. The responsiveness of the industry to the broad priorities and charters depends, to a large extent, on the needs of the industry and on the respective ministry's ability to service these needs.

Four, consensus is an ongoing process. It requires constant interaction, which is achieved through joint consultative committees (*shingikai*) and trade associations. In order to obtain consensus, the Ministries must often act as conciliators, if not also as arbitrators at times. The latter role is performed primarily through administrative guidance.

Five, consensus should be unanimous. As such, much negotiation, discussion, and persuasion (both formal and informal) must take place before a final decision can be reached on an issue.

Industrial Policy

Japan's industrial policy is best understood in terms of the operations of the policy (i.e., the administrative process) rather than in terms of the policy itself (i.e., the legal and legislative process). The Japanese bureaucracy considers that, at the level of the individual firm, market forces should be allowed to operate. At the level of the industry, however, the Japanese government believes that it has an important role to play in terms of the redistribution of capital and labor and in the promotion of technological development (see Abegglen 1982).

REFERENCES

Abegglen, James. "Industrial Policy." In *Japan and Western Europe*, edited by Loukas Tsoukalis and Maureen White, pp. 43-55. London: Frances Pinter.
Kiyoaki, Tsuji, ed. 1980. *Public Administration in Japan*. Tokyo: University of Tokyo Press.

2 GOVERNMENT-BUSINESS RELATIONSHIPS IN THE UNITED STATES AND JAPAN
A Comparative Analysis

Mitsuaki Sato

Much has been said and written about the economic performance of Japan and how it contrasts with that of the United States. However, many of these comparative analyses have suffered from one common limitation, namely, a failure to view the goals and records of the two countries in the context of their respective histories and geographies. A prime example of such a misconception is the so-called phenomenon of "Japan Inc." which was fostered in the United States in the past decade. Under this interpretation, Japan is viewed as a huge business-government complex the goal of which is to sell its products overseas and the operational headquarters of which is the Ministry of International Trade and Industry (MITI), where I have worked for the past twenty-six years.

Let me briefly compare our two nations: The United States is the ultimate frontier country. Of all the great nations, it is the one with the greatest margin of safety for experiment, whether for economic opportunity or for political self-government. Secure between two oceans, the United States is a vast land mass abundant in natural resources; however, it has always needed to import human resources. Now turn to Japan. It is a bleak offshore archipelago that, ever since it set out to be more than a subsistence economy, has had to devote much of its talents merely to buy the most basic raw materials from abroad.

This is not to say that there are not many parallels between U.S. and Japanese economic history. Like Japan, the United States has had to encourage and protect infant industries. For twenty years, for example, Pan Am grew as "the chosen instrument" of U.S. greatness in the air. A whole generation of Americans has grown up forgetting that the Republican party had traditionally espoused a policy of imposing stringent tariffs. Today, the U.S. grain industry would certainly feel the chill if it did not have many friends in Washington.

What I wish to propose here is that although there is certainly a greater degree of coordination between government and business in Japan than in the United States, the relationship is quite different from that suggested by the concept of "Japan Inc." I would also propose that, in common with the United States, the vitality of the private sector is the mainspring of economic growth in Japan.

In Japan the core of government-business interaction is encapsulated in the industrial policy. One can say that Japanese industrial policy both reflects and shapes the government-business relationship. Industrial policy has become a controversial subject in the United States. On the one hand, it has become a subject of debate in U.S. trade deficits with Japan, where some argue that industrial policy is responsible for distorting two-way trade in Japan's favor. On the other hand, industrial policy has also become a domestic issue in the United States as both academicians and politicians have debated whether or not Japan's experience has any relevance to America's revitalization efforts.

Considering that vital matters such as U.S.-Japan trade and America's revitalization efforts are at stake, it is unfortunate that there is much misunderstanding about Japan's industrial policy. Such misinformation and misperceptions not only create new difficulties but also delay and hinder the solution of existing problems.

Let me clarify what industrial policy really means in Japan. Historically, Japan was a latecomer to industrialization. In a short span of time the country had to catch up with the West. This necessitated the government's playing a direct, developmental role from the very beginning of the modernization effort which began in the second half of the nineteenth century. The government built steel mills and textile factories which were then sold to the private sector. Such measures have left a heritage of interdependence between the government and business. This does not mean that the Japanese businessman always agrees with the bureaucrat. In the United States the businessman is known to say: "I am all for the free market, except for my own industry." Something similar can be said of the Japanese businessman. The Japanese businessman, however, believes the State has to undertake the important functions of facilitating economic development and enhancing welfare. Also, he has long accepted the idea that the government is responsible for remedying certain inadequacies in the market mechanism, particularly in terms of coping with long-term, structural problems.

Japan's industrial policy in the post-World War II era can be divided into two broad phases. During the first phase, which lasted until 1960, the government not only coordinated overall planning but also intervened in the operation of individual enterprises in order to improve their efficiency. Such positive assistance provided by the government is referred to as the policy of industrial rationalization or *sangyo gorika seisaku*, which was implemented to help rebuild Japan's economy, which was devastated during the war. During this phase the government adopted the following measures to foster economic recovery: the imposition of import restrictions to protect infant industries; the regulation of access to capital; the granting of direct subsidies, research and development subsidies, and tax benefits; and export development.

After 1960, as Japan's economy was rebuilt, such direct assistance was gradually eliminated and emphasis was shifted to establishing goals and priorities for various sectors of the economy. This new phase was designed to facilitate the transformation of the economic structure. In order to determine which industries should be emphasized for strategic development and which should be phased out gradually, various criteria have been used, including the income elasticity of demand, comparative production costs, labor absorption power, environmental impact, and investment effects on related industries. In carrying out these measures, MITI has played an important role by proposing, every ten years, a set of macroeconomic goals or what is referred to as a "vision" for the nation.

The differences between the two phases of postwar industrial policy indicate the overall decline in direct government controls on private industry during the last thirty years. There are a number of reasons for this decline. During the first decade or so after the war there was a clear and strong national consensus that priority should be given to economic recovery. This consensus served to justify the need for strong government leadership in economic matters. The eventual success of the recovery lessened, however, the need for an authoritative government role; and what had been a solid consensus on national goals weakened as growth for growth's sake came to be questioned. Furthermore, the liberalization of trade and capital during the past two decades has helped reduce the government's direct leverage over industry.

Perhaps more important, Japan's economic growth in recent years has brought considerable economic power to certain sectors of the economy and, with it, a tendency to be more assertive in promoting industry or company interests, whether or not they are in the overall national interest. One recent example is the well-publicized differences of opinion between MITI and the automobile industry on the question of voluntary restraints on exports to the United States. MITI wanted to prevent disruptions in the U.S. market by allowing Japanese car manufacturers to export as many cars as they wished, whereas the auto manufacturers argued that as long as President Reagan wanted the voluntary export restraint terminated and the U.S. consumers wanted to buy Japanese cars, there was little need to be dictated by political pressures. In the end, the auto industry agreed to compromise, but only after a series of intense negotiations with MITI. In a similar situation at an earlier time, MITI would have relied on its legislative power to enforce its will.

I do not want to underestimate the extent to which the Japanese government, especially MITI, can influence business today through statutes and regulations. There are also various forms of direct financial assistance to certain industries, specialized tax incentives, and financial controls. They are, however, limited to large-scale R&D projects, pollution, regional development, and other areas where the private sector alone cannot be expected to meet the needs of the public. Furthermore, such measures are not very different from the incentives and restrictions that prevail in many other nations, including the United States.

Besides the aforementioned evolution in Japan's industrial policy, there are several issues pertaining to government-business relationships that should be mentioned. First, Japanese business respects the government for its competence. The prestige enjoyed by the Japanese government is evidenced by the fact that the civil service continues to attract graduates from top-grade universities. This is especially true of MITI and the Ministry of Finance, both of which play a predominant role in economic matters.

Second, MITI assembles high-quality information and utilizes it in its policymaking process and administration. Third, in general, business believes and trusts that MITI is truly concerned with its welfare. Fourth, MITI places considerable emphasis on maintaining good communication with business and into consensus building. For example, over 200 consultative committees have been established to maintain a regular exchange of views between bureaucrats and corporate leaders from various sectors. In addition, in formulating MITI's "visions" on long-term macroeconomic goals, the government makes an utmost effort to ensure that the views from business, labor, the media, and the academic world are represented.

It should be noted, however, that consensus building is not always harmonious and that consensus is sometimes not achieved. Even at the height of MITI's influence in the early postwar period, some companies went their own way and defied government policies. Honda Motor Company, for example, refused to work with MITI in the 1960s when the agency tried to persuade it to stay in the business of manufacturing motorcycles and not to expand into the production of passenger cars. MITI did not want another company to enter into the auto industry. Another example is Sumitomo Metal Industries, Ltd., which flatly refused to follow MITI's guidance, which was aimed at avoiding excessive increases in the steel industry's production capacity. Defying the government agency's wishes, Sumitomo pushed through its enormous investment programs. Nowadays, it is not uncommon for a particular segment of business to be in open disagreement with the government. As a recent example, I mentioned the case of MITI versus the automakers with regard to voluntary export quotas.

This leads me to another important point, namely, the great vitality of Japan's private sector. Although the role of the government in laying the groundwork should not be overlooked, it was the private sector that really accomplished Japan's so-called economic miracle. The dynamism and strongly capitalistic spirit of Japanese industry are manifested in the intense competition that prevails within most industrial sectors. This is a phenomenon to which foreign scholars have often pointed. To ignore it would be to seriously misinterpret Japan's recent economic history.

Still, the cooperative relationship of government and business remains a distinctive feature of Japan's economic experience. A combination of historical, cultural, and natural factors are conducive to this type of relationship. These factors are: the prestige of the government, as mentioned earlier; a high degree of social homogeneity; a strong emphasis on social harmony and consensus; group loyalty; subordination of the individual to the group; and a tendency to rely on the government for allocation of scarce natural resources and space.

If one gives weight, as I do, to the importance of such factors in formulating Japan's industrial policy, it follows that the Japanese model has little relevance to the United States because of its very different political and economic cultures. As has been pointed out elsewhere, the United States has a long history of adversarial relations between government and business as well as between business and labor. Although there is some evidence that the American attitude toward government-business relations is changing, any attempt at revitalization in the United States must take fully into account the major characteristics of America's own experience, which is very different from that in Japan.

Nevertheless, it is imperative to have a correct understanding of Japan's experience for several reasons. First, by understanding Japan's case and through comparative analysis with the Japanese experience, the United States can gain a better insight into its own situation, which may provide ideas for an American-style industrial policy. Second, the widespread misunderstanding of Japan's industrial policy and government-business relations tends to unnecessarily complicate U.S.-Japan dialogue on trade problems and may even threaten bilateral relations. Third, this misunderstanding of Japan may divert U.S. attention from the important task of fully realizing the great economic potential of the United States.

In conclusion, I would like to affirm that each nation has the right to chart its own course of development based on its particular needs and traditions. Japan's government-business relations and industrial policy are natural and evolutionary outgrowths of Japan's history, society, and natural endowment of factors of production. At the same time, however, as economic interaction among nations becomes closer and more intense, it has become more and more difficult to isolate domestic economic policies from such matters as trade, assistance, cooperation, investment, and so forth. That Japan's government-business relations and industrial policy have become a factor in bilateral trade frictions illustrates this phenomenon. Evidently, then, approaches to economic development must have an international perspective as well as the ability to meet domestic needs and goals.

I believe that Japan meets the required standards of fairness and international mindedness. But it is probably true that in order to avoid misunderstanding, Japan needs to do a better job of clarifying its distinctive industrial policy and government-business relationships. Meanwhile, however, the United States will hopefully give more attention to achieving its goal of revitalizing its economy rather than blaming the domestic economic policies of other countries, such as Japan's industrial policy. With such mutual efforts, we should be able to realize a prosperous future.

3 COMPARATIVE ASPECTS OF THE GOVERNMENT-ENTERPRISE INTERFACE IN THE UNITED STATES AND JAPAN

Howard F. Van Zandt

This chapter provides a comparative analysis of the historical evolution of government involvement in industry between the United States and Japan from the seventeenth century through the present. The following historical perspective facilitates our understanding of the present nature of government-enterprise relationships in the respective countries.

JAPAN: SEVENTEENTH TO EARLY TWENTIETH CENTURY

During the Tokugawa era (1600-1868) Japan was divided into *han* or clans. Commercial enterprises of substantial size were very often operated under the auspices of the *Daimyo* (feudal lord) of the *han*. By the time Commodore Perry arrived in 1853 the tradition of government control of business was strong, and businessmen had come to accept it. This does not mean, however, that all businesses were directed by the government. Retail shops were privately owned and managed, as were inns on the nation's major highways. Money changers performed some of the functions of bankers.

In the early part of the seventeenth century foreign trade was usually dominated by the powerful *Daimyo*. The *Daimyo* profited from this trade and eagerly sought the opportunities that came with the foreigners. The Spaniards and Portuguese often insisted that the *Daimyo* and their clansmen become Catholic as a condition of trade. If the *Daimyo* did not agree, the traders would take their business elsewhere.

When the first Americans came to Japan in May 1791 at Kushimoto Oshima, their efforts to commence trade were rebuffed. Neither the *han* government nor the Tokugawa leaders in the capital city of Edo would allow American commerce to take place. Over the course of the next sixty-two years—that is, until the arrival of Commodore Perry—about 1,000 Americans were known to have visited Japan. However, all efforts to open trade through official channels were firmly rejected. During this same period many other Americans visited the coast of Japan and engaged in trade privately and, from the Japanese standpoint, illegally.

When the country was at last opened to the world in the summer of 1859, foreign commerce was allowed but only under the supervision of the government. For a quarter of a century, efforts to build modern industry were, to a considerable extent, financed and directed by the *han* or the national government. By the 1880s, however, these enterprises were, with few exceptions, turned over to private hands. These private businesses came to be known as *zaibatsus*. Needless to say, the bureaucracy followed closely the activities of the *zaibatsu*.

As private business developed its own managerial and financial skills, the government reduced its supervisory activities. Much of the success of the Japanese private sector was due to the guidance and advice given by foreign bankers, businessmen, engineers, and scholars, especially during the period 1865 to 1923. My grandfather, George Van Zandt, a Chicago banker, was invited by Japanese capitalists to go to Tokyo in the early 1870s to establish a bank. He thought about it for two to three years and studied the Japanese language, but he finally turned down the offer because he was then rising within his bank in Chicago. My father, Paul C. Van Zandt, had much to do with building a modern cement industry in Japan while serving as chief engineer of the Asano Portland Cement Company from 1918 to 1923. There were thousands of others who were like my father and grandfather.

During the Taisho era (1912-1924), government interference was far less than before or since.

AMERICA: SEVENTEENTH TO TWENTIETH CENTURY

In colonial times commerce in the colonies was ostensibly conducted in such a way that the mother country would benefit. The Spanish, English, Dutch, and French governments tried to restrict the trade of their respective colonies with colonies that belonged to other European powers. They also tried to prevent their colonies from direct trade with other European countries. However, given the great distance between Europe and the American colonies, it was difficult to enforce the mercantile system of foreign trade monopolies. As a result, the colonists often engaged in what might be termed "innocent smuggling of necessities." The relationship between the colonial governments and the colonies deteriorated as a result, and the American Revolution and revolutions in Latin America against Spain ensued.

Evolution of Relationships between Government and Business during the Great Depression

In Japan governmental controls were adopted during the Great Depression as an effort to create employment. The military interventions in Manchuria and China that followed thereafter further intensified the need for government involvement in business. World War II witnessed the culmination of the dominant role played by the government in all aspects of economic operation. Japan was in such poor shape at the end of the war that the Allied Occupation authorities could not dismantle the bureaucratic apparatus, but instead transferred power from the military and industrial wartime mobilization units to peacetime bureaucracy. The Ministry of International Trade and Industry (MITI) was created in May 1949. One of the basic characteristics of bureaucracy in Japan is that it is devoted to giving practical guidance and help to its people. The public knows this and is appreciative. The result is business-government cooperation and harmony.

The United States stumbled badly during the Great Depression, and the Franklin D. Roosevelt administration put government into a strong position in numerous areas. Theoreticians in Washington propounded their ideas and demanded that the nation follow the principles they laid down. In the accompanying social revolution Supreme Court justices set up their own moral concepts, and the public was forced to abide by them.

Often the new principles enunciated by the Washington theoreticians did not work. The morals preached by the Supreme Court frequently were no less impractical. As a consequence of history, and the ascendancy to power by bureaucrats and judges, disharmony between government and business increased.

The Japanese were spared new principles and new morals. Nakamura Hajime of Tokyo University once declared: "The characteristic feature of Tendai Buddhism in Japan consists of emphasis upon things rather than principles." Dazai, a Japanese Confucianist scholar, sneered: "I would rather be a master of acrobatic feats than a moralist."

SOME PERSONAL EXPERIENCES

In general, Japanese firms knew that their government's policies were to give practical, sensible advice and help, and they were therefore more willing to follow governmental directives in the form of administrative guidance. Numerous vehicles were created to facilitate communication between government and business. These included the trade associations, rural cooperatives, and political organizations.

Japanese companies, if left to themselves, were excessively competitive and the resultant price wars threatened to destabilize the affected industries. To prevent calamity, MITI and other agencies had to face the feuding industrialists and make them raise prices and reestablish sanity in their marketing activities.

Japanese government agencies sometimes pointed out foreign technical developments to private companies and advised them to obtain licenses from abroad to get into promising new fields of endeavor. The bureaucracy facilitated this by erecting a host of new tariff and nontariff barriers to protect the firms that were entering into the new businesses. These barriers were maintained long enough so that the domestic companies could become large and through the economies of mass production meet foreign competition both at home and abroad.

Despite promises made by Japanese officials to complaining foreign governments, impediments to entry of foreign products and services continued. One of the reasons lay in the lifetime employment practices of government ministries. Bureaucrats who had devised these new and ingenious means of keeping foreign products out were not dismissed when the restrictive measures were removed. Rather, they stayed on and devised substitute measures with the same objective: "Keep the foreigners out."

In a meeting at the Embassy Residence in Tokyo a half dozen years ago, I was a member of a group including high officials of the Ministry of Foreign Affairs, MITI, and the embassy. The topic was: "How should the mounting complaints made by U.S. businessmen of unfair actions taken by Japanese officials be handled?" I proposed the appointment of an ombudsman who would receive the criticisms and see that justice was done. In time, the Japanese government did create an "Office of the Ombudsman." Unfortunately, to date, the trade ombudsman has lacked the authority to bring unfair bureaucrats into line.

The American Embassy in Tokyo is fully aware of the seriousness of the huge and ever-growing deficit in U.S.-Japan trade and extends help to U.S. firms. However, there is only so much that can be done. The American Chamber of Commerce in Japan also plays a leadership role in trying to persuade the Japanese authorities to really open their markets. I was president of the American Chamber of Commerce in Japan at one time and served on its Board of Governors for fifteen years. I believe that the chamber, through its score of committees and activities designed to train Americans and nudge the Japanese government to be more conciliatory, is performing a very valuable service.

STRATEGIC PLANNING FOR THE FUTURE

U.S. government-sponsored research will continue to be directed largely toward defense and the space industry. On the other hand, Japanese government efforts may be expected to focus on the development of commercial products and services, including aerospace. As long as these policies continue, the United States is liable to suffer from huge trade deficits.

The Japan External Trade Organization (JETRO), a government agency, recognizes the need for Japan to increase its imports from the United States and other countries and hence strives to teach foreigners how to reach the Japanese market. This is a good strategy for Japan because if the trade imbalances continue to grow, it is inevitable that restrictions will be imposed on the import of Japanese products.

Americans should not expect Japan to open the door to U.S. agricultural products much wider than it is at present. Japanese strategic planners recognize that if all restrictions on food imports were lifted, Japan's dependence on foreign agriculture would soon rise to 70 to 80 percent of their food needs. This would result in an unacceptable level of risk, particularly since the United States is the chief source of foreign food now, and its prospects for continued food surpluses are not bright.

The problems the United States faces in agriculture are well known to Japan's long-term planners. First, there is the problem of water shortages. The Ogallala Acquifier in West Texas, New Mexico, Oklahoma, Colorado, Kansas, and so on has for many years supplied an abundance of subterranean water for irrigation. It is drying up rapidly, and when it is empty a vast part of the nation's breadbasket will no longer be irrigable. Second, there is the problem of soil erosion. Vast portions of the nation's richest farmlands have been overcultivated for so many years that the depth of the soil has dropped to a dangerous level. For example, land in Illinois and Iowa, which had rich three-foot-deep soil some fifty years ago, is now in the sad situation where the soil is only three to six inches deep. Third, there is concern that illegal and refugee immigration will innundate the country and consume whatever food surplus might have been available for export. Mexico is the largest source of illegal immigrants. In 1984 alone, it was estimated that well over 1 million had escaped from the border patrols and will remain illegally in the United States. Mexico's problem of high population growth is grave indeed. In 1940 its population was only 19.6 million. By 1980 there were 80 million Mexicans, about 10 million of whom were in the United States, mostly illegally. Estimates put Mexico's population at the range of 126 to 145 million by the year 2000. Food experts believe that Mexico can produce only enough to feed 54 million people adequately. What will happen when there are 126 or 145 million people? Inevitably, there will be revolution as the hungry fight each other for what scraps they can find. This will result in a tremendous influx of refugees and illegal aliens into the United States, estimated to total 25 to 50 million by the year 2000. Fourth, there may be political turmoil in the United States resulting largely from the spillover of Mexico's troubles. When Mexico is enwrapped in the throes of a civil war, the people who are in power will be threatened by those who fled the fighting and moved to the United States. Much of this fighting will spill over across the border. Cities such as San Diego, Los Angeles, Phoenix, Tucson, El Paso, Midland, Odessa, San Antonio, Corpus Christi, Laredo, Harlingen, McAllen, and Brownsville may be caught in armed strife. A way—probably the only way—to avert this possible calamity would be to erect a wall along the U.S.-Mexico border stretching from the Gulf of Mexico to the Pacific. Japanese planners know that, and they realize that Americans are basically short-term planners and will not take protective steps until it is too late. They do not want their fellow Japanese to go hungry because of American shortsightedness.

SOME PROBLEMS IN STRATEGIC PLANNING

Because they lack a sufficient domestic supply of oil, iron ore, and countless other raw materials, the Japanese are dependent upon political conditions in foreign countries. The success of their strategic plans is therefore contingent upon the stability of conditions in the supplying nations. Japanese strategic planning does not only depend on distant countries as sources, but it also relies on foreign nations to remain financially solvent, politically sound, and affluent enough to pay for Japanese products. The Japanese feel that their government is doing what it can to benefit, protect, and look after the interests of the Japanese people in its relations with foreign countries.

Americans have far more raw materials than most countries and are better able to meet their own needs. However, even the United States is dependent upon foreign nations for many essential minerals. One complication to U.S. strategic planning is that the nation is, because of its military strength, frequently involved in the disputes and troubles of distant countries. These political/military problems cannot be foreseen and often wreck whatever plans have been made. As such, U.S. companies and farmers never know when Washington will suspend trade, even though temporarily, with some countries.

Americans do not have the group consciousness of the Japanese. U.S. subsidiaries abroad increasingly employ local nationals and reduce American expatriate staffs. For example, a U.S. computer joint venture in Japan has 4,000 employees, only one of whom is American. He is not even the president of the firm. Japanese firms feel that their purpose in being is to benefit Japan, and the most obvious way to do this is to create good jobs for Japanese people. The president of Japan's second largest bank told me that his bank would never lend money to a Japanese company operating abroad that gave the best jobs to foreigners.

The decline in the competitiveness of U.S. firms overseas in the past ten years is due, in no small measure, to poor strategic planning. Companies have pulled back their expatriates and appointed local nationals to replace them. Communication problems have become much more worrisome than before. Also, there is no longer much foreign service experience/expertise in U.S. corporate headquarters. My success in living and working abroad was often dependent upon the cooperation of people back in the United States who had lived previously in the Orient and who knew from personal experience what the problems were. Now this supply of former expatriates is dwindling to a dangerously low level.

STRATEGIC ISSUES FOR GENERAL TRADING COMPANIES

4 THE UNCERTAIN FUTURE OF JAPAN'S GENERAL TRADING COMPANIES

Stefan H. Robock
Kichiro Hayashi

Recent environmental forces have been eroding the traditional competitive advantages of the Japanese general trading companies (GTCs). As a result, the central strategy issue facing the GTCs is how to retain their competitiveness by adapting to the new forces and by developing new competitive strategies.

Although the Japanese general trading company is basically a merchant trader whose income derives mainly from buying, selling, and distributing goods, its traditional competitive advantages arise from combining other valuable functions with the trading function in versatile and efficient ways. In a recent article (Hayashi and Robock 1982), we have selected six major competitive advantages of the GTCs as a conceptual framework for assessing the future importance of the Japanese general trading companies. These functional advantages are as follows:

1. The financing function;
2. The trading and transportation efficiency function;
3. The information function;
4. The risk-bearing function;
5. The negotiating and organizing function; and
6. The direct investment function.

Each of these functions is examined below.

THE FINANCING FUNCTION

The GTC can perform a valuable financing function for its customers because of its unique access to domestic and foreign bank credit. Domestically, the base of the GTC's credit worthiness lies in its past payment performance, its well-established diversification, and its industrial and banking group affiliations. In foreign countries the GTCs have become well known and enjoy a top credit rating in New York and other world financial centers. Next to the leading Japanese banks, the GTCs have easiest access to Eurocurrency markets and other foreign financial sources.

The financing function is not a direct source of profit to the GTCs, however. The usual interest rate charged is not commensurate with the risk involved. The additional profit to the GTC is expected from the incremental trade that results from performing the financing function.

GTC financing is particularly in demand by small firms to which domestic and foreign lenders are not willing to lend directly and by manufacturers in highly cyclical industries. Typical examples of the latter are the sugar industry and the steel companies which were brought under GTC control during the 1962–1965 recession.

The development by the GTCs of important financial functions was largely a result of the slow internationalization of major Japanese private banks, called the city banks. During the 1950s and 1960s the international expansion of Japanese banks was tightly controlled by Japan's Ministry of Finance. By 1970 the ten city banks allowed to deal in foreign exchange and the Bank of Tokyo, designated as the bank that specializes in foreign exchange, had established only fifty-eight overseas offices in all. Furthermore, their international business services were extremely limited, consisting mainly of simple export-import financing. During this period the GTCs greatly strengthened their position in foreign trade and as joint international investors by providing to Japanese firms financial services that filled the international banking void.

After 1970 an international takeoff period for Japanese banks began. In response to Japan's continuing favorable balance of payments, the Ministry of Finance reversed its restrictive control policy and encouraged capital outflows. Japanese firms began a wave of foreign direct investment expansion, creating new demands and opportunities for banks in international finance.

By 1977 Japanese banks had reached a high level of internationalization based on global networks. Including a semipublic bank, the Industrial Bank of Japan, they had expanded to 111 branches, 57 subsidiaries, and 299 offices of representatives overseas. Leading securities firms, such as Nomura, Nikko, Daiwa, and Yamaichi, had turned their attention to overseas markets and established an international network of about seventy outposts in twenty countries. Also, the Ministry of Finance had helped establish three so-called flag-led consortia, one in Paris and two in London, to avoid excessive competition between Japanese banks in these strategic locations. The extent of internationalization of Japan's banks can be illustrated by the case of the Bank of Tokyo which had 40 percent of its deposits accounted for by overseas deposits in 1978 and 80 percent of its profits coming from overseas—proportions that were comparable to leading U.S. banks.

These environmental changes mean that foreign exchange banks can now provide more adequate financing for international business, thus possibly taking over part of the financing functions of the GTCs. Also, the banks now have their own global networks that permit them to acquire information on business opportunities, independently of the GTCs. One leading city bank reports that 80 to 90 percent of the overseas information leading to business opportunities is acquired independently of the GTCs. Also, the banks are in a better position than the GTCs to investigate the credit worthiness of a prospective foreign buyer. When buyers' credits are available the GTC can receive immediate payment. This means less risk. It also means less leverage and likely lower profits.

In the area of import usance, the GTCs have had an advantage over banks in Japan in financing prepayments and loan-purchase investment funds to overseas materials suppliers through the ability of the GTCs to borrow from foreign banks. Now the overseas subsidiaries of Japanese banks can perform this function on more favorable terms because the top ten Japanese banks have a higher credit rating in international financial circles than the GTCs.

In financing direct foreign investment, Japanese manufacturers used to rely on the GTCs to arrange finance from the Export-Import Bank of Japan and the Overseas Economic Cooperation Fund as well as from foreign sources. Now they are more likely to receive assistance from the internationalized Japanese banks. For example, a Japanese manufacturer of rubber products recently established a sales subsidiary in the United States and chose to finance this expansion through the U.S. subsidiary of a Japanese city bank rather than through a leading GTC. As a result, the manufacturer will probably reduce its future trade business with the GTCs. Many more Japanese firms are likely to follow this pattern.

Many GTC executives, however, appear either optimistic or unaware of the creeping challenge from the banks. They view the internationalization of banking operations as beneficial to the GTCs in terms of financial convenience or information. Furthermore, they are convinced that there always are enough Japanese manufacturing and mining firms in the international markets that the banks would rather finance through the GTCs, as is the case on the domestic scene. This may well be so. But does this mean that the GTCs will end up specializing in less favorable industries, as is the case with, for example, the sugar, electric, and open hearth furnace industries on the domestic scene?

In addition to the challenge of the Japanese banks, many Japanese firms have become better known to foreign banks and in foreign security markets and have developed direct access to non-Japanese sources for financing.

TRADING AND TRANSPORTATION EFFICIENCY

The GTCs can perform the trading and transportation function at a low cost as a result of the size, scope, and synergy of its operations. The rate of commission charged by the GTCs may be as low as 0.2 percent.

The GTCs are diversified in products and markets. They deal with tens of thousands of different goods in 120 four-digit industries. Each GTC is represented in more than 100 countries. This diversification, supported by the information network, highly qualified personnel, and ownership interests in many overseas resource development projects, have made the trading and transportation services of the GTCs extremely efficient. As of 1977 the "Big Nine"[1] together

---

1. The "Big Nine" companies include Mitsubishi, Mitsui, Marubeni, C. Itoh, Sumitomo, Nissho-Iwai, Tomen, Kanematsu-Gosho, and Nichimen.

were investors in 179 natural resource projects which create international flows of materials traded by the GTCs. The group also had 24 processing, warehousing, and/or distributing terminals overseas.

A GTC can provide many valuable services for an inexperienced Japanese manufacturer when it first expands internationally. The GTC can offer effective expertise in conducting feasibility studies, negotiating with prospective local partners and governments, making financial arrangements, and setting up logistics frameworks for multinational procurement of components if needed for local production. However, as the manufacturer gains experience in foreign production, foreign marketing, international financial markets, and so on, the firm may wish to break away from the GTC. This means that the GTC's strategy must cope with constant changes in products, sources of supply, and markets. In depicting the future profile of the GTC, the question arises as to whether such a trend will eventually weaken the international role of the GTC as compared to the major role it has played in the recent period of Japan's industrial internationalization.

What are the reasons advanced for the gradual and eventual separation of manufacturers from the GTCs? First, the GTC frequently lacks detailed technological know-how. As a result, GTCs' salespeople need help from the manufacturer's engineers to design ingenious marketing programs and to sell technologically sophisticated products. If they are required to participate heavily in marketing to keep their products moving satisfactorily, the manufacturers eventually feel they may just as well do it themselves. An additional advantage of direct participation in foreign markets is more rapid feedback on technical characteristics of the products. Examples of products in this category include electric appliances, electronics, pharmaceuticals, and machinery.

The second reason for separation relates to weakness of the GTCs in consumer marketing. Many manufacturers of consumer goods initiated their foreign business activity with GTC collaboration but then became dissatisfied with the GTC's marketing program after the initial period. Since the GTCs rarely create house brands for consumer goods, seldom develop their own channels, and do not have a necessary network for service and the sale of parts, the transition in marketing control from the GTCs to manufacturers is not difficult. For instance, Japanese auto manufacturers turned away from the GTCs well before their sales volume reached large proportions.

Third, in some cases, the GTCs themselves wish to separate from manufacturers because the arrangement is unprofitable for the GTCs. The volume of business may not be large enough, as in the case of specialty steel, to justify the involvement of the GTC even in the U.S. market. Similarly, a product might not allow adequate commission or might be too difficult to sell.

Thus, the pattern of transition can be summarized as follows: First, the larger and more significant the market, the sooner the manufacturer turns away from the GTC. For example, C. Itoh still handles auto marketing for Toyota in Saudi Arabia. Second, the more complex the technology involved, the sooner the manufacturer turns away from the GTC. Third, the more specific and involved are the marketing and service requirements, the sooner the manufacturer turns away from the GTC.

These patterns imply that the GTCs eventually would specialize in fragmentary markets, technically unsophisticated products, marketing-free consumer goods, and industrial products (such as capital equipment made to order) that require their global network. Large development projects such as the building of superports or industrial parks and the export of complex plants are additional examples of foreign operations that require GTCs' organizing capabilities as well as their information networks. Some GTCs are developing internal technical teams to enhance their technical capabilities for large projects and to collaborate with multinational engineering firms such as Bechtel. Other firms, such as steel manufacturers, cannot separate from the GTCs entirely because they depend on the GTCs for raw material import. Japanese steel mills still export and invest overseas to a significant extent in collaboration with the GTCs. Some GTCs have developed and engaged in consumer marketing in textile products, foods, and several other items, but it seems unlikely that this will develop into their major strategy in the near future.

THE INFORMATION FUNCTION

The information function deserves special attention. It is based on global information networks and personnel well versed in foreign markets. And it goes well beyond usual market information. It may involve finding joint venture opportunities for the GTC customers anywhere in the world. It may be as specific as identifying the international consultant for a certain foreign project that will shortly come up for international tender. The information function may facilitate a combination deal where Sri Lanka would like to buy a machine if it can pay in rubber. The GTC can locate a buyer for rubber through its global network so that the Japanese exporter can receive payment in cash for its machine.

In information scanning, the GTC's unique asset is its human resources. And the strength of the information function hinges critically on the traditional lifetime employment policies because these practices minimize knowledge leakage. Currently, the GTCs are under strong and growing pressure to employ local nationals, to share local ownership (which also means hiring local nationals), and to internationalize their central management. To the extent that the localization pressures result in nonpermanent employment policies, they seriously weaken a primary source of competitive advantage for the GTCs.

The examples of foreign environmental pressure for localization of personnel and for local sharing of ownership are legion. In Southeast Asia and the Middle East local pressures have reached the point where employment of parent (home) country personnel often is legally prohibited or tightly controlled by restricted issuance of work permits. In South Korea, for instance, the GTCs are required to hire four Koreans for each Japanese. Even the United States has exerted localization pressures through its equal opportunity employment laws and by restricting the issuance of visas for Japanese employees of the GTCs.

The response of the GTCs has been to hire local personnel and to organize some joint ventures with a minority ownership. The question for the future is: How far can the expatriates-locals proportion be pushed before the information system is seriously threatened? The answer lies in the nature of the information function and the problems associated with relying on local managers for informational work.

The information function has two major components. One is general background information, such as economic and political trends in major countries and the trends of major multinational corporations. The second is business-specific information that could lead to specific business transactions. The general information is usually collected and analyzed by corporate staff and normally does not depend heavily upon locally stationed personnel. Business-specific information is more critical for the GTCs and depends mainly on locally stationed personnel. In relying on non-Japanese local personnel, the GTCs encounter several categories of problems, namely, the difficulty of attracting superior talent in the local markets, information leakage, and communication difficulties mainly due to language.

The GTCs have difficulty attracting superior talent in both the industrialized and the less developed countries. In the industrialized countries prospective employees do not view the Japanese GTCs as offering long-range career opportunities for non-Japanese. In the less developed countries availability of the necessary talent is seriously limited. In either case, even if promising individuals are available, it is questionable whether they will stay with the Japanese firm long enough to become fully effective in informational work. The past record has shown that university-trained managers require at least seven years' work experience, a devotion to the accumulation of knowledge, and strong entrepreneurial attributes to become well qualified for the informational function.

The most difficult requirement for locals is knowledge of the GTC's numerous collaborative affiliates in Japan and intricate relationships with Japanese competitors. Without this knowledge, the overseas staff cannot know what information is useful and how information should be presented. A complex custom-made "systems project" in particular requires extensive and well-integrated knowledge. An example is the Iran-Japan petrochemical project organized by Mitsui wherein the latter was able to bring together more than eighty Japanese firms to participate in a joint venture. Many local nationals do not stay with the GTC long enough to become proficient in this organizing function.

The information leakage problem has recently received much attention in the United States, especially in the high technology industries of Silicon Valley. Some brave experts have even estimated that as much as 50 percent of business-specific information that has obvious value and application may be lost to a firm through leakage. In the United States a common form of leakage is through employee turnover. In certain developing countries leakages occur as a result of rebates and kickbacks (also known as bribery) which are difficult to control. Japanese managers abroad are a protection against both types of risks. They plan on lifelong careers with their companies and hence are not likely to risk their careers by accepting bribery benefits.

The communications problem involves both language and cross-cultural relations. To solve the language problem, some firms have attempted to use English as the sole medium of communication in foreign subsidiaries, but without lasting success. Most Japanese feel awkward using a foreign language to communicate with another Japanese. Many senior executives at headquarters lack a solid command of English. As a result, letters and memorandums that contain nuances and intricacies must be written in Japanese. Many telexes are sent in Japanese for fear of miscommunication or leakage, or simply out of laziness.

In cross-cultural communications lack of familiarity with Japanese customs can be a decisive factor in preventing immediate intercommunication of quickly perishable information with the most appropriate party.

How are the GTCs attempting to adapt to the new environmental pressures in the information area? They have developed training programs for selected foreign managers, including bringing them and their families to spend twelve to eighteen months in Japan at company expense to receive on-the-job training. They have programs to internationalize headquarters managers by sending them on business trips overseas, to language schools, to foreign business schools, and to executive development programs in Japan and abroad (Tung 1984). Some GTCs have adopted a policy not to use Japanese in telex communications. Another policy is to pair a Japanese manager with a local manager to blend two sets of knowledge to the best advantage. But the success of these measures in preventing the erosion of the competitive advantage in the information-scanning function is still highly uncertain.

DIRECT INVESTMENT FUNCTION

As of May 1979 the "Big Nine" general trading companies had made equity investments in about 1,360 overseas projects, almost always as a minority participant with another Japanese company. The GTCs have been attracted to most overseas joint production ventures as minority investors primarily for incremental trade benefits. They gain short-run profits from handling the export of capital equipment for establishing the project. Over the long run they normally gain continuing profits by handling the trade in parts and component inputs for the foreign operation and the export of finished products. Often, overseas projects have been a defensive strategy to avoid the total loss of a foreign market for finished goods.

The GTCs' competitive advantage in the direct investment function is based on their ability to identify opportunities in many product and market areas, their negotiating and organizing capabilities, their financial strength, the availability of experienced personnel that can help staff the projects, and the GTCs' extensive affiliations with industrial groups.

The share of labor force with university degrees is relatively small in most Japanese manufacturing and mining companies. In contrast, well over 80 percent of the GTC male employees are university graduates, and the ratio has been increasing in the 1970s. As of 1980 the GTCs had a total of almost 40,000 male employees who had an average of 15.1 years of in-house training. Even the largest Japanese manufacturers find it impossible to match the experience and training of GTC personnel. These employees are highly experienced in varying combinations of products, foreign trade, commercial laws, credit, ocean and land transportation, foreign exchange, finance, accounting, foreign markets, and so on.

In moving from a trading to a direct investment function, however, the GTCs have encountered serious limitations. As Professor Yoshino concluded in a study, once a venture gets underway and the trading pattern is settled, both the GTC personnel in the venture and the headquarters' product division lose enthusiasm for the operations aspect of the venture. Yoshino (1976: 122) argues that "the product division staffs had neither time, temperament, nor expertise to undertake feasibility studies" for overseas manufacturing ventures and for going beyond the trade sphere.

The poor GTC performance in overseas manufacturing ventures has also been explained by an opportunity cost concept. The GTCs incur an estimated annual cost of up to $220,000 per male employee stationed overseas, including costs up to retirement. This is 1.4 times the cost of his domestic counterpart. Many small-scale manufacturing joint ventures simply fail to live up to the GTC's internal opportunity cost of using scarce personnel.

For the future the crucial problem of the GTCs in implementing the direct investment function is that the GTCs have not focused on developing production managers, because production management is the responsibility of the manufacturing or mining partner and not the GTC.

OTHER FUTURE ISSUES

Two other future issues should be briefly noted. In the organization area the traditional global product division structure of the GTCs is being strained under the strategy requirements for managing multiple products and multiple functions in numerous foreign markets. As a result, the GTCs are more or less coping in various ways with problems of interproduct division communication (Hayashi and Robock 1982). The other issue might be labeled "domestic goodwill at bay." The GTCs have encountered adverse currents in their domestic environment and so far have not succeeded in completely reversing them.

CONCLUSIONS

This brief survey of selected strategy issues facing Japan's general trading companies is not a valid basis for drawing sweeping conclusions as to the future of the GTCs. As one Japanese authority has said: "The obituary of the *sogo shosha* has been written many times." These comments should not be construed as still another obituary. The GTCs are aware of these strategy issues and are continually redefining the domain of their business activities.

In the medium range of five to ten years, changes in the GTCs' profiles will continue to be evolutionary rather than revolutionary, despite the flood of new environmental forces. Material changes in the basic characteristics of the GTCs are unlikely, but significant modifications in certain GTC functions should be expected.

First, the information- and boundary-spanning functions will continue to be reshaped by the inevitable transition from ethnocentric to geocentric orientation in staffing. The increased pool of local and international personnel should stimulate third-country trade and investment that spans non-Japanese boundaries. In contrast to the past when Japan has been the hub, boundary spanning and the GTC's information network will become more internationalized and global in nature. Japanese personnel, however, will continue to deal with perishable business-specific information relating to activities that span Japan's national boundary, either directly or indirectly. An example of indirect spanning would be exports to the U.S. market from a Japanese firm with production facilities in the Philippines.

Second, the historical trend of the GTCs toward ever more product and market diversification may be somewhat reversed. GTCs may be forced to specialize in less technically demanding products, relatively marketing-free consumer goods, industrial products that require global information scanning, and fragmentary markets. Some areas likely to emerge as GTC specialities include foods, forest products, fuels, metals, and special-order facilities and equipment. This reverse trend may not progress to the point that it will destroy the GTC's leverage in risk diffusion, combinational trading and transportation, and the project organizing function. Nevertheless, some smaller GTCs may become less versatile in offering these services and eventually may be forced to change their basic characteristics.

Third, the internationalization of Japanese financial institutions may not financially weaken the GTCs themselves, but the growth in alternative sources for financing will reduce the GTC's finance function as a means of obtaining international business. Where risk is big, the GTC will still serve as an important source of funds. Thus the GTC finance function may shift heavily in the direction of risk bearing. The information function may also change, the financial institutions replacing the GTCs as specialists in international credit information.

Fourth, in the organization area, the GTCs are more or less coping with problems of interproduct division communication through the use of coordination staffs, top management committees, matrix teams, and "centers" of experience such as a plant export center. The strengthened regional headquarters in North America and Western Europe can maintain consistency in regional interproduct strategy, if they are cautiously adjusted for unfavorable side effects. In the intermediate future, the strategy of strengthening regional headquarters will be extended beyond North America and Western Europe, as the other areas grow in importance as sources of raw materials and markets for special-order facilities and equipment.

The formal grid structure, widely used in many non-Japanese international companies, will not become prevalent in the GTCs for two reasons. One, strategy typically is not developed at the top level and implemented by the middle echelon in Japanese firms. Two, extensive informal communication already occurs almost as if a grid structure existed. The Japanese approach, therefore, for reducing sectionalism will be to place emphasis on personnel behavior through the "revolution of consciousness" rather than on changing formal structure. Some devices to promote the revolution of consciousness may develop, such as a system of positive reward for forming new interproduct and project teams.

In sum, the most essential characteristic of the GTCs will become increasingly recognized as that of national boundary spanners, but including investment and many other arrangements as well as trade. The GTC will be engaged in any business that promises returns higher than existing per capita opportunity costs. The push toward *global* spanning will come from increasing pressure to localize personnel in foreign posts, the consequent growth of the third culture group within the GTC, and increased competition among the GTCs. Increased competition has already become so severe that some GTC activity has slipped into socially questionable areas. If Japanese economic growth slows down, there may not be enough potential spanning business for the nine GTCs, and this will create an incentive for the GTCs to modify their basic concept of raison d'être.

REFERENCES

Hayashi, K., and S.H. Robock. 1982. "The Uncertain Future of the Japanese General Trading Companies." *Kajian Ekonomi Malaysia* (December): 45-67.

Tung, R.L. 1984. *Key to Japan's Economic Strength: Human Power*. Lexington, Mass.: LexingtonBooks, D.C. Heath.

Yoshino, M.Y. 1976. *Japan's Multinational Enterprises*. Cambridge, Mass.: Harvard University Press.

5 STRATEGIC ISSUES FOR THE *SOGO SHOSHA*

Hiroshi Kohiyama

To a visitor from Mars the relationship between the United States and Japan would undoubtedly appear at times as a confused sort of game, an "Alice in Wonderland" version of baseball played with oranges and aluminum bats, where the winners sit down to beef dinners and the losers' children sweep up the other side's computers. Even Tug McGraw would have a hard time believing this one.

But, like Mr. McGraw, I am an optimist. Beyond the rhetoric and the persistence of some real problems, the substance of our bilateral relationship is one of dynamic interchange. The opportunities for new growth—for both competition and cooperation in carving out new areas of endeavor—abound as never before. The increasing trend toward the internationalization of design, production, and distribution; the fast pace of economic development in the Pacific Basin; and exciting advances in new technology on both sides of the Pacific have made the U.S.–Japan connection a particularly fertile territory for growth and expansion. It is in this context that Mitsubishi and other integrated trading companies are sorting out and acting on the strategic issues that confront them.

One obvious issue arises from the changes in the business environment itself. As you know, through the end of Japan's high-growth era, the *shosha* functioned and prospered as commission traders dealing largely in bulk commodities, and as suppliers of information, financing, and marketing know-how to a wide range of manufacturers engaged in both domestic and international sales. Partly as an extension of these trading activities, we also engaged in natural resource development and organized major international construction projects. While all of these remain basic to the functions of the *shosha*, in recent years a number of factors have combined to change the overall outlook and strategy for the future.

The end of the high-growth era in Japan was accompanied by a leveling off in trading volumes. Japanese manufacturers who once relied on the *shosha* for their overseas marketing now learned to do the job themselves. Trade conflicts resulted in limited revenue growth in areas of traditional strength, such as steel. Competition for market share of what was often a shrinking pie began to squeeze traditional margins. It became apparent that even before the start of the 1980s, a new approach was called for.

With this change in the business environment, we realized that we would have to become more than just commission merchants. In order to grow we would have to be active investors, product distributors, and business organizers—not simply in terms of the Japanese economy but on a multinational scale. Even in traditional trading areas, there was clearly going to be more stress on offshore transactions, such as Canadian pulp and South American coffee beans to the United States, and selling American heavy equipments to the Middle East. Today, in fact, U.S. subsidiaries of Japanese-based *shosha* rank among the top exporters of U.S. goods to the world marketplace.

Another area into which we have moved is countertrade. In recent years, because of the currency reserve problems of debtor countries, there has been an increase in countertrade activities throughout the world. The *sogo shosha* are particularly well set up to handle such countertrade transactions. Out of numerous types of countertrade, I would like to select and illustrate counterpurchase, buy-back, and switch transactions, using cases we have recently encountered and dealt with successfully.

In 1982 Mitsubishi was the first Japanese company to enter into a contract under the Indonesian government's counterpurchase policy. The arrangement called for us to ship 200,000 tons of fertilizer to Indonesia, one-third of which were exported from the United States. In return, an equivalent amount of Indonesian products, such as aluminum, were imported into Japan. In counterpurchase the export and import transactions were conducted in two separate but related contracts, each involving cash settlement.

A few years ago we sold a plant to East Germany for manufacturing fluorescent lamps. The arrangements called for us to undertake the international marketing of the output. The bulbs are now being sold in neighboring European countries.

We have recently exported U.S. products, fertilizers in this case, to Brazil under a switch arrangement which would route payment through East European countries. By taking advantage of the imbalance in the clearing account between Brazil and Hungary, our sales to Brazil were made possible; otherwise they would not have been. Hungary was pleased with the switch transaction because it partially offset the imbalance of their clearing account with Hungary. Brazil was satisfied because it could import foreign products without expending its hard currency reserves.

In sum, because of the size and diversity of operations of the *shosha*, we are able to handle these complex types of countertrade transactions. If we have to buy butter in order to sell machine tools, we have a product division that knows where to find the bread as well.

A third area into which the *sogo shosha* has moved is the provision of a more comprehensive and flexible array of services to established industries that are undergoing transition. These services include the supply of technology, equipment, and new materials as well as project financing to established industries. Where appropriate, we seek a constructive role in the "high-teching" of the smokestack industry itself. In the United States, for instance, we have been supplying advanced German/Japanese-made continuous casters to several major steel manufacturers, along with customized financial packages.

In general, it is in the application of advanced technology to established industries and in the creation of new knowledge- and technology-driven industries that we see the greatest opportunities for future growth. In our view, it is significant that the process of developing and commercializing such technology has become increasingly international in scope.

In the area of high technology we have tried to adopt a three-dimensional approach that utilizes our established resources to meet the demands of the new marketplaces that are emerging. For example, Mitsubishi recently acquired equity in a company called Microrim, a software manufacturer based in the state of Washington. As agent for the company, we have also forged a link-up with a Japanese software developer who can make linguistic and other necessary modifications to adapt Microrim's products to the Japanese market. In Japan Mitsubishi has also tied up with IBM and a Japanese software-oriented venture company to develop and market information hardware and software. These are aimed primarily at the Japanese telephone monopoly's plans to build an integrated information network system that covers homes, offices, factories, stores, and even highways.

For more than ten years we have acted as the sole representative in Japan for the contract research services of Ohio's Battelle Memorial Institute. Conversely, we also have an arrangement with the Research and Development Corporation of Japan to market and promote new Japanese technology in the United States. In fields such as office automation and medical equipment, we are working with U.S. high technology companies to import certain sophisticated components under original equipment manufacturer (OEM), including financing and other aspects. Mitsubishi has created new working units within the company to facilitate the matching and exchange of technologies and to pursue opportunities for direct participation in terms of investment, finance, and marketing. Although these pursuits still account for a relatively small proportion of our company's revenues at this time, we anticipate substantial growth in these areas.

Another area into which the *shosha* has moved is the direct marketing of manufactured goods. The limitations on the role of invisible "matchmater" and the tangible rewards of forward integration have served as the motivating forces to move in this direction. In the U.S. market, for example, Mitsubishi has been strengthening its sales activities through the establishment of a number of distribution subsidiaries and joint ventures. As a case in point, Mitsubishi Electric recently formed a new company with Stromberg-Carlson, known as Astronet. The purpose of the new company is to produce and market a cellular mobile telephone system. With other partners, we are also engaged in the sale of Mitsubishi cars and giant screen diamondvision systems which are installed in sports stadiums and other sites. We have also established our own distribution subsidiaries in a number of fields, such as canned goods and construction equipment. Recently, we established a coil-processing subsidiary which will supply new computerized technology to both U.S. and American-based Japanese customers.

In fiscal year ending March 1985 the direct marketing of manufactured goods accounted for 6.229 percent of Mitsubishi's total consolidated trading transactions. See Table 5-1.

Table 5-1. Mitsubishi's Trading Transaction in Manufactured Goods, March 1985.

MC FOODS—canned goods	84,935,866
Coil plus	39,300
Non Ferrous International Corporation	28,719,093
PALMCO	111,392,912
The RJM Company	10,297,014
Bensenville—machinery tools, mobile phones	47,321,055
General Merchandise Division of Mitsubishi International Corporation total	220,052,530
RUB Division of Mitsubishi International Corporation total	4,720,790
Textile Division of Mitsubishi International Corporation total	99,833,827
Astronet	332,621
Wire and Cable Co. Inc.	28,987,699
Diamond Plastics Corporation	19,921,920
FAMSA	—
Machinery Distribution Inc.	84,280,897
Tubular Services West Inc. (tubular)	3,263,122
Total summarized from above (A)	744,098,646
Total consolidated trading transactions (B)	11,945,791,229
% (A)/(B)	6.229%

In addition, we have made substantial investment in resource development in the United States. Several years ago we joined with the Kennecott Corporation to modernize and then share ownership and production in that company's Chino, New Mexico copper mine. Our objective was to make the Chino operation the world's lowest cost producer of copper. Mitsubishi has sought to market most of its share of the refined copper here in the United States.

Our portfolio also includes an oil exploration subsidiary, grain elevators, and a number of other investments. Our aim, of course, has been to establish deeper roots in the U.S. economy. Strategically, we are seeking to become a more truly multinational enterprise, providing not only a window to Japan but a range of services and resources to partners all over the world. Clearly, the United States is going to continue to occupy center stage in that effort.

In light of all the aforementioned changes, there is little doubt in Mitsubishi's minds as to what directions should be taken in the future. However, the new strategies continue to pose challenges to the *shosha*'s organization and corporate culture. I will outline what we have done in this regard.

In Japan, Mitsubishi Corporation was reorganized in order to streamline decisionmaking and to redeploy human resources in areas where we see the greatest prospects for new growth. In its annual recruitment of college graduates, the company is hiring a far greater proportion of applicants with technical qualifications and, in a major departure from past practices, is now hiring some particularly qualified people out of other organizations.

Similar changes have been made in our overseas subsidiaries, such as Mitsubishi International. As I said, our goal is to become a creative enterprise with a permanent presence in international markets and industries. In short, we seek to develop a modernized and "Americanized" version of the *sogo shosha* which participates in economic activities in the United States in ways that parallels our parent company's role in Japan. To achieve this goal we have expanded significantly our U.S. office network. In the past the *shosha* were basically positioned in port cities where they could direct the flow of goods into and out of the continent. We wanted to move inland where the industries and the markets are. In the past several years, we have established new offices in Atlanta, Philadelphia, Denver, St. Louis, and most recently, Minneapolis. While these operations start out as mini-branches, we expect them to develop into significant sources of new business in the future.

To support their efforts and those of the established branches, the company has also made some organizational changes. The intention has been to strengthen the regional management system, coordinate ongoing activities, and systematize the pursuit of new business, particularly in the area of high technology.

In the personnel area we have seen the need to recruit and develop more American managers—qualified and motivated people who can help create and run the company's "Americanized" business. To this end we have revised the compensation system, instituted formal management development programs, and launched a program of two- to three-year assignments for qualified Americans at the parent company in Tokyo.

We, of course, view this as a long-term project, but we are cautiously optimistic about the results.

Caution, it has been suggested, is of the very nature of a *sogo shosha*. Certainly, no one can deny that we have just come through a very difficult period and that more hard times may lie ahead. Last year this occasioned a revival of the *shosha* obituaries that have been penned on and off since the first oil shock in 1973-1974. The integrated traders, it was suggested, had entered their "winter age" and were unlikely to see another thaw. Whether this is so, or whether a combination of new strategies and new growth cycles will bring us around to another spring remains to be seen. At this point, however, I would answer, along with Mark Twain, that "reports of our demise have been greatly exaggerated."

6 STRATEGIC ISSUES FOR THE GENERAL TRADING COMPANIES

Thomas B. Lifson

The *sogo shosha*, or Japanese general trading company, is an institution unique to Japan. It is also a fairly difficult type of corporation to understand, given its diversity of products and functions. In studying the *sogo shosha*, I have developed two models, or organizing perspectives, to understand better the key strategic issues that face a *sogo shosha*.

In defining the strategic issues for a *sogo shosha*, one must first explain, in a parsimonious manner, what it is that a *sogo shosha* really does. My way of explaining what a *sogo shosha* does is to say that it manages "product systems." In the jargon of business strategy, its key success factor is its ability to manage product systems. What then is a product system?

A product system consists of producers of goods and services that perform all the types of operations necessary to transform raw materials into finished products in the hands of their ultimate consumers. It is a fundamental characteristic of industrial society that practically everything we use has passed through many hands on its way from original raw materials to us. A product system is a way of identifying those groups of companies and individuals who systematically work together over time, channeling flows of information,

---

Parts of this chapter are based on M.Y. Yoshino and T.B. Lifson, *The Invisible Link: Japan's Sogo Shosha and the Organization of Trade* (Cambridge, Mass.: MIT Press, 1986).

money, physical goods, services, and other economic goods to place end products in consumers' hands.

Two examples will allow me to explain better. The first example is historically the first type of product system managed by a *sogo shosha*: the cotton textile product system. Cotton textiles were not only the first Japanese industry to mechanize and export, but there is also a long history of extensive cotton textile manufacture and trade in Japan. It takes many producers and middlemen to get cotton from the fields to people's backs, as it were. Figure 6-1 presents only a few categories of the principal types of actors that are involved in this industry.

Note the different basic stages of production; raw materials; primary processing in spinning; further processing in dyeing, weaving, and other operations; and finally to downstream activity such as wholesaling, apparel manufacture, and retail sales. It is a characteristic of this industry that many of the producers in this sytem are relatively small businesses. Almost everywhere, but particularly in Japan, companies prefer certain vendors and customers and deal regularly with them. Ties of credit, information exchange, and other sorts of relationships often develop between pairs of these producers.

A system of interdependencies links the producers in this product system. Their fates are bound together by the health of the whole system. If cotton supplies cannot be obtained on reasonable terms, they all suffer. If competitors elsewhere start using an improved weaving process that lowers costs and improves quality, unless the current weavers in the system can either make the same improvements or are replaced, all will suffer. These small specialized firms that are members of this product system usually do not have the resources, information, personnel, money, or perspective to see the system as a whole and manage the whole system.

A *sogo shosha* is a type of firm that manages these sorts of product systems as a whole. In fact, in the nineteenth century the *sogo shosha* were active in assisting Japanese producers to import cotton, machinery, and technology to facilitate the development of the cotton textile industry in Japan. Textiles, along with the metals industry, became the prototypical industrial sector for future diversification by the *sogo shosha*.

Today the six largest *sogo shosha* are involved in virtually all of the basic industrial sectors: food, fiber, metals, chemicals, energy, transport, machinery, finance, electronics, and information. Usually,

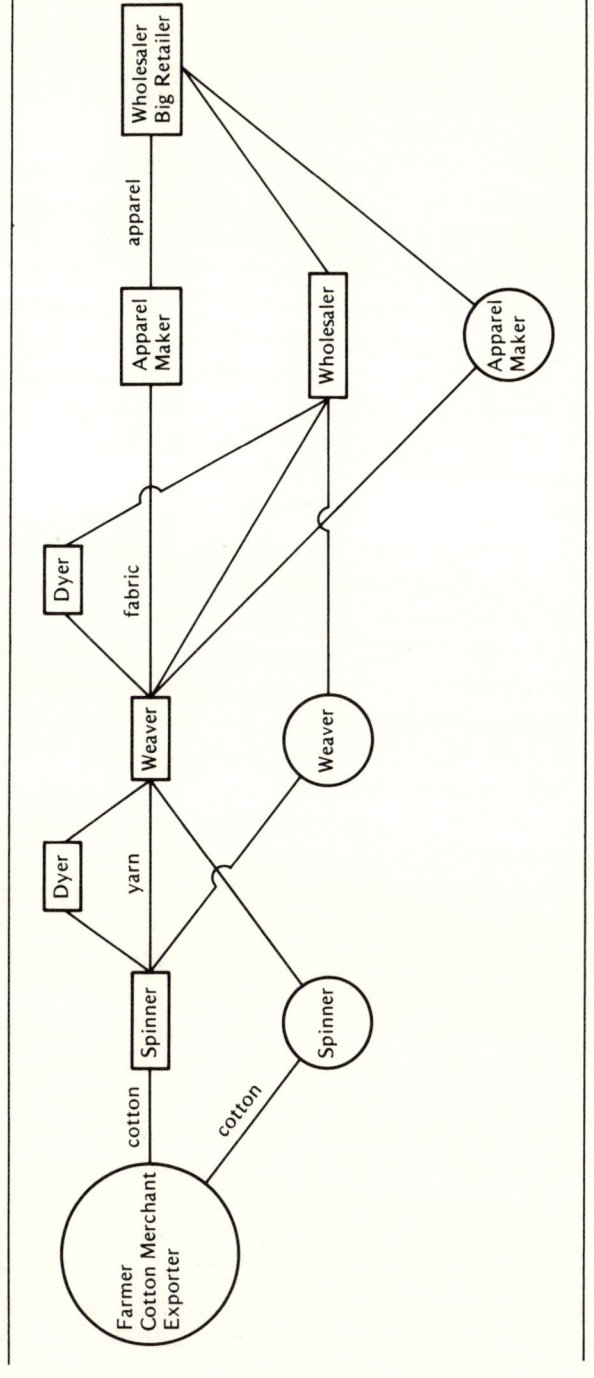

Figure 6-1. Some Types of Actors in the Cotton Textile Product System in Japan.

a *sogo shosha* will manage the flows of goods from raw materials, through the hands of several specialized producers or vendors, all the way downstream. Usually, a *sogo shosha* will have an ownership position in only a few of the operations. Often, this ownership is a minority stake.

As was pointed out in chapters 4 and 5, the *sogo shosha* typically makes minority equity investments in the case of metals. I have looked at the nonferrous metals business. In many of the resource-producing countries, the government requires the foreign firm to invest in local mines or processing facilities as a precondition for doing business. Most natural resource investments are aimed at stabilizing flows and gaining bargaining leverage. Some natural resource investments may return substantial profits and some may not. The purpose of the investments lies in strengthening the *sogo shosha*'s role in the total system.

The overall reason as to why the trading companies are becoming more active in foreign direct investment is their attempt to manage the total system. They need to have an equity share at various stages. Strategically, on average, the distribution system is where you get the most "bang for the buck," so to speak, in terms of influence and leverage over the total system. At other stages, however, they must also get involved not as vertically integrated, wholly owned producers on the model of the River Rouge Works of the Ford Motor Company, but as partial owners and as exercisers of influence through not only equity shares but the provision of financing, information, logistical services, and so on.

Whether there is a trend toward greater equity ownership and more control of the system by the *sogo shosha* is difficult to say because it varies from product to product. In some cases, there is more ownership. For example, in the textile industry there is more ownership because customers are undergoing such financial pressures that they either go under or they have to be recapitalized. In declining industries one sees greater *sogo shosha* ownership, although it is not a voluntary management policy. In expanding industries they start from a low base and may increase as an investment in the future.

In Figure 6-1 some of the actors are represented with rounded rather than square shapes. These represent companies in which a *sogo shosha* might have an equity interest. Of course, in actuality, any *sogo shosha* deals with hundreds of actors in a product system. There are many more types of actors who provide specialized outputs, and there are often many firms providing the same outputs who all deal with the *sogo shosha*.

A second example comes from the petroleum industry. Figure 6-2 presents a highly simplified version of some aspects of the petroleum industry in Japan. Here again, we see that complex flows are the pattern.

There are many competitive strengths to be garnered by managing a system like this *as a system*, instead of as a collection of individually acting companies. For one thing, in-process inventories can be drastically reduced. For another, response to change can be coordinated. Finally, there may be operations in which economies of scale beyond the reach of a single firm can be exploited.

In exchange for managing the system as a whole, and for bringing them specific benefits, the members of the system pay fees to the *sogo shosha*, usually based on volume. One of the things a *sogo shosha* may do in return is to help the members of the system adjust to change. In the textile industry, for example, the *sogo shosha* have managed the transfer of wool weaving out of Japan. Sometimes they have been involved in helping Japanese weavers, who are clients, establish joint ventures in lower wage countries, using Japanese expertise and machinery and local management and labor.

However, if things are stable for a long period of time, and clients do not perceive the *sogo shosha* as protecting them from risk, then the longer the clients work together, the less need will the other members of the system tend to feel they have for the *sogo shosha*. They learn about each other; they gain experience and the ability to manage some key variables among themselves. Inevitably, they put pressure on the *sogo shosha* to lower its fees. They can threaten to take their business elsewhere or handle the services currently being provided by the *sogo shosha* themselves; that is, they can vertically integrate. Eventually, the revenue that the *sogo shosha* receives from the entire product system declines.

Figure 6-3 traces the patterns of revenue of a *sogo shosha* in a product system. Point A is the theoretical point in time when a *sogo shosha*'s involvement in a product system begins. In practice it would be difficult to pinpoint any such moment. At that juncture an investment in time (axis AY) and resources (axis AX) begins for the *sogo shosha*. Revenues usually do not begin to flow in until later, at point B. Revenues increase and can catch up with expenses at point C. The horizontally shaded area ABC represents the net upfront investment

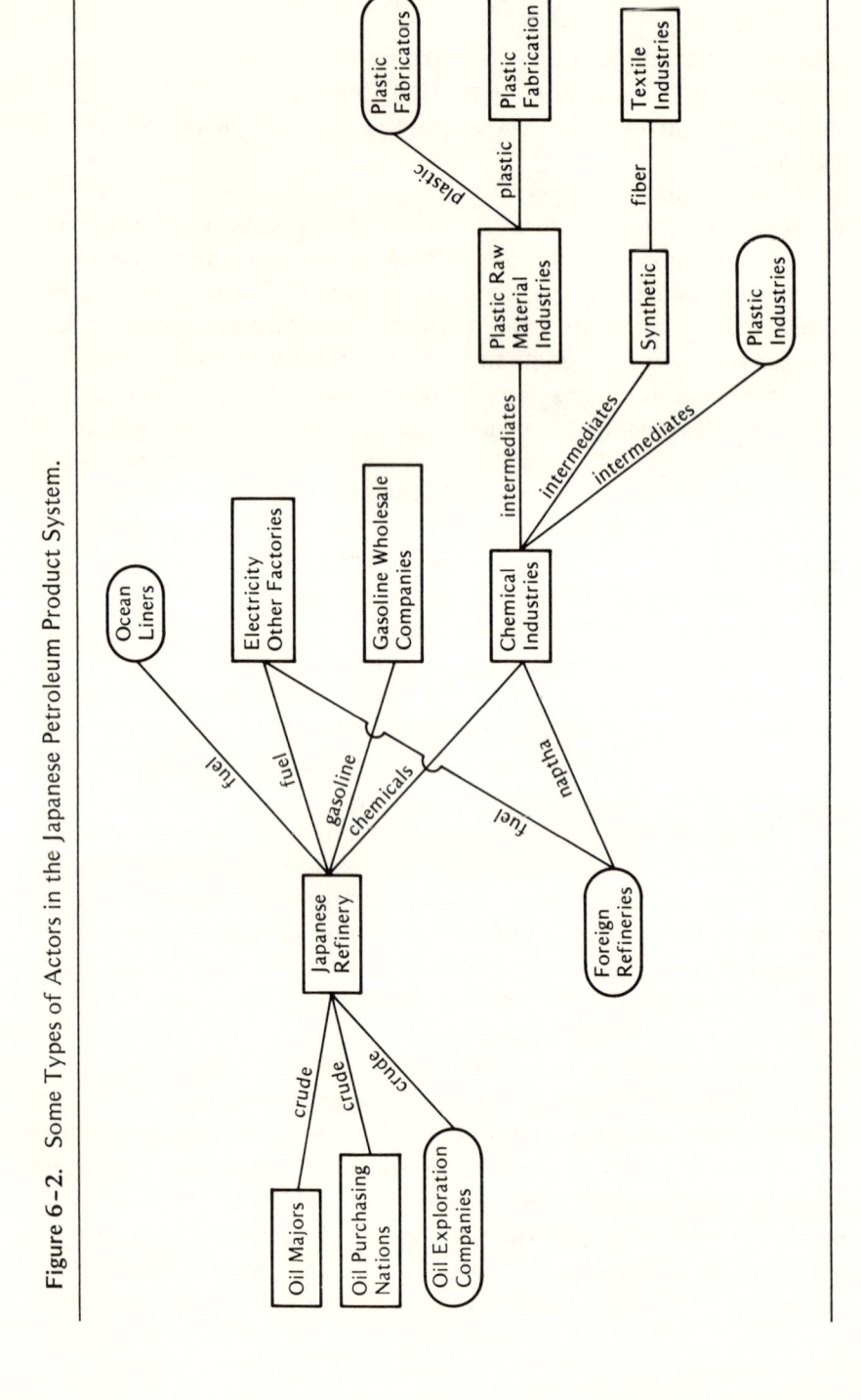

Figure 6-2. Some Types of Actors in the Japanese Petroleum Product System.

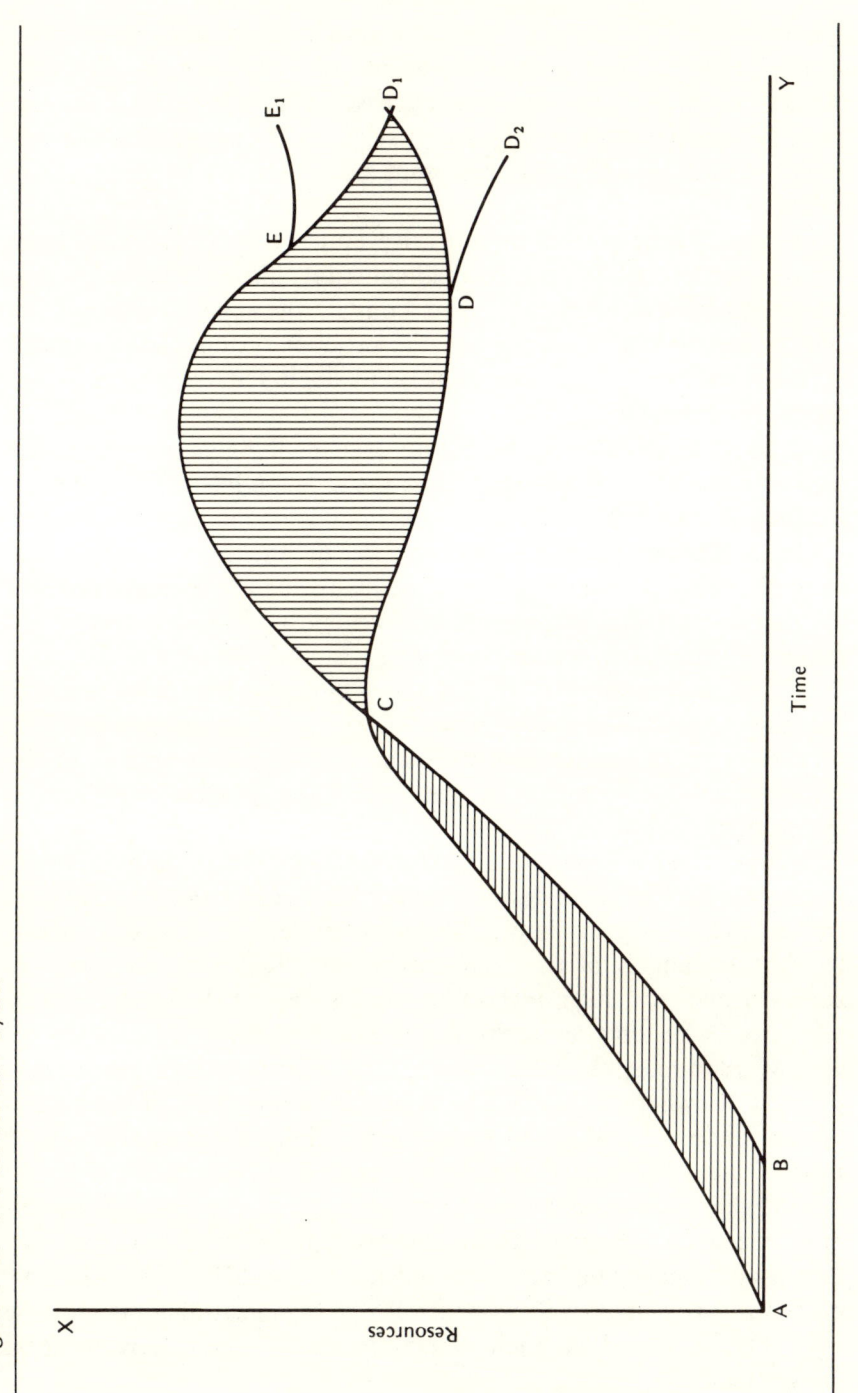

STRATEGIC ISSUES FOR GENERAL TRADING COMPANIES 61

Figure 6-3. The Service Life Cycle.

in resources which the *sogo shosha* makes in establishing its position in the system. After point C it begins to make money. The *sogo shosha*'s costs may or may not decrease, while the revenue may or may not continue increasing. But a *sogo shosha* hopes that the vertically shaded area CD_1 will represent a substantially larger sum than ABC.

Eventually, the system matures. Revenues drop as pressures from clients, and probably from rival or substitute product systems, lowers overall system profitability. At point D the *sogo shosha* may decide to increase its investment in the product system (line DD_1), or decrease its investment (line DD_2) and deploy its resources in another product system.

At point E, which may be before or after D, revenues may either recover (line EE_1) or not (ED_1). In the balance lies the future profitability of the system management function for the *sogo shosha*.

Using this perspective I would describe the *sogo shosha*'s key strategic issues as follows: First, too many of the existing product systems are mature, stagnating, and generating low or negative net resources, much less return on invested capital. Structural change in the Japanese economy since 1973 has hurt the *sogo shosha* badly because it has affected most adversely the product systems in which they were most heavily involved. The most dynamic sectors of the Japanese economy today as yet have only modest *sogo shosha* involvement.

Second, the expense necessary for the *sogo shosha* to build up its position in new product systems is very large, and it takes a long time for returns to flow in. Thus, the net investment necessary to ensure the future viability of the *sogo shosha* looks large. This is especially true because the high technology industries—such as electronics, information systems, biotechnology—into which the *sogo shosha* are aiming, require specialized training and talents, which are in high demand elsewhere in Japan. The *sogo shosha* must recruit young university graduates and spend many years training them as *sogo shosha* professionals. They have already begun to do so in a major way, but it will take some years before these recruits are able to create significant business for the firm. In the meantime the technologies and markets may be changing very fast, and it may be difficult for the specialists to keep up. It will be a formidable organizational task for the *sogo shosha* to adapt their organizations to these new business environments.

A third and possibly bigger challenge awaits, as the *sogo shosha* adapt their organizations to function well in developing another vitally important growth opportunity perceived by the *sogo shosha*, namely, their overseas subsidiaries. But here too the obstacles are formidable. This is a complex subject on which I have published elsewhere (Lifson 1981). It is sufficient to note that the localization of overseas operations to enable them to do more effectively for overseas clients what the *sogo shosha* have long done for domestic clients will be a complex, long, difficult, and expensive but necessary process. In many countries it is a political necessity as well as a business opportunity.

Although there are grave difficulties ahead for the *sogo shosha*, some individual firms will survive a restructuring of the industry. A smaller number of healthy *sogo shosha* may be able to generate enough net revenue to adapt themselves to a useful and profitable role in the global economy. It is not a certainty, but the *sogo shosha* have survived far more perilous times than these and have emerged stronger than ever. It would be premature to write them off today. Their survival depends on the abilities of the companies themselves to manage another great transition in the history of this unique institution.

REFERENCES

Lifson, T.B. 1981. "Mitsubishi Corp. (B)" 9-482-051. Boston: Harvard Business Case Services.

7 U.S. TRADING COMPANIES
Corporate Organization for Countertrade

Thaddeus Kopinski

U.S. firms are encountering heavy competition in most markets these days, and this competition is complicated by a global liquidity problem. That is, many of the markets to which U.S. firms want to sell do not have currency with which to pay. In more and more cases, these markets are demanding various sorts of barter, offset, and compensatory trade arrangements, collectively called countertrade; such countertrade requirements force U.S. firms to develop a competitive response. They must learn to trade under this system and hence develop the appropriate organizational form to handle these complex trading activities.

Many firms begin by engaging an independent trading house to handle their countertrade obligations. After several years of mounting commission and subsidy payments to the independent houses, many firms elect to develop an in-house trade capability. This takes time. Executives who have presided over the creation of trading companies state that one to two years may be necessary to establish a smoothly functioning operation, to say nothing of a profitable operation.

In looking at the potential corporate setup for handling countertrade, it is important to differentiate the primary purpose of a com-

Excerpted from T. Kopinski, *Threats and Opportunities for Global Countertrade* (New York: Business International Research Report, 1984).

pany's trading operation, the major ones of which are listed below: Is it primarily a service unit chartered to dispose of parent company obligations—thus effectively an extension of corporate marketing strategy? Alternatively, is it primarily oriented to fulfilling a financing role, either to provide creative financial solutions to boost direct exports and to gain market share or to reduce company or bank credit exposure particularly in countries with high commercial or sovereign risks?

The growing imposition of tighter import controls by many less developed countries (LDCs) is effectively impeding normal multinational corporations (MNC) trade flows or making them more uncertain. Some MNCs are finding themselves excluded from these markets for an indefinite period when the products they sell are refused import licenses. A recent case in point is Rockwell International, the sales of which to Latin America plummeted by 65 percent last year, particularly in its automotive division. "Countertrade is not the answer, but it is a partial and temporary solution," a company executive told Business International. It is noteworthy that the company's countertrade obligations globally rose from 2 percent of total foreign sales in 1980 to 12 percent in 1984.

One option traditionally used to hurdle such barriers has been to transfer production capacities to the countries that restrict imports. However, manufacturing on the spot is not always economically viable, particularly in many of the least developed countries. It is also not an option that is likely to be chosen at a time of economic austerity. Thus, many multinationals are seeking other alternatives. Countertrade offers a viable solution, enabling companies to negotiate an import quota with the government of the country that imposed the controls in return for commercial advantages of equivalent value, that is, the option to purchase or export local products.

The experience of one large European food manufacturer is typical of what firms are beginning to do. According to company executives, this firm does not regard countertrade as an end in itself and would prefer to do without it. However, it manufactures a wide variety of food products in 280 factories located in 55 countries. Over 90 percent of its turnover is derived from products manufactured in the country of sale and consumption. Nevertheless, some finished or intermediate products have to be imported because, for reasons of efficiency, their manufacture cannot be decentralized. Since several of the countries where the firm is established have encountered economic and monetary difficulties, it has increasingly had to resort to countertrade transactions and has set up a special management unit for this purpose at its head office.

The European firm cites the following reasons in this context:

1. To enable some of the factories relying on imported components and packaging, machinery, or spare parts to operate continuously;
2. To maintain market shares and the presence of brand names in countries that have interrupted normal imports;
3. To develop new markets for its products in countries where there is no possibility of penetrating by other means;
4. To facilitate payment of dividends, royalties, and so on to the parent company; and
5. To create a favorable business climate for itself in the country in question.

Another example is provided by a North American manufacturer of agricultural equipment which found its traditional Latin American markets shrinking because of customers' difficulties in obtaining foreign exchange. With recession in the Western countries, the firm turned to LDC markets. Though the demand was there, the means were not. As in the above example, the firm set up a countertrade department specializing in purchase and resale of primarily agricultural products, such as coffee, tomatoes, and canned goods. It has thus been able to turn around what promised to be a disastrous situation.

Some of the more aggressive and experienced multinationals are initiating countertrade proposals when financial settlements are blocked because of exchange controls in the partner country. They negotiate so-called advance purchases with an escrow account in a third country. This account records the value of the transactions of both the firm and the debtor country. The assets side would show the purchases of countertrade products that would offset liabilities and even keep up the flow of deliveries that would otherwise have been suspended owing to nonpayment.

Countertrade is also helping to expand available credit by enabling a bank to bypass country limits and country credit risk evaluation. One trading house interviewed by Business International concluded a deal in which a commercial bank issued 80 percent of a transaction value in a loan to the trading house, the remaining 20 percent of the credit being taken by the trading house itself. The risk was thus on the trading house and not on the country and end-buyer of the countertrade deal. This trading house strongly recommends that multinationals offer countertrade as a backup if the LDC cannot obtain or cannot absorb the cost of normal export financing. "Such a prenegotiated countertrade alternative should clearly have the LDC importer pick up the cost of the subsidy and the trading house fee," this trader noted. "Presenting such alternatives not only shows the MNC's goodwill, but also makes the LDC aware of the cost involved in doing business the countertrade way."

Countertrade is also being used as a financial technique to help repatriate blocked funds or remit frozen dividends, particularly in a number of Latin American and Southeast Asian markets. Although a limited number of such transactions have been successfully completed, most falter over the question of official versus parallel exchange rates and the risk of devaluation. As one executive told Business International in reference to his operation in Brazil: "The only way you are going to get your dividend out is to earn the cash to do so in hard currency—and now is the time to do it." Other experiences entail (1) purchase of real estate or nonfixed assets for local currency and resale in foreign exchange outside the country or in countries where this is possible and (2) the purchase of forward contracts to get dollars at the official rate at a stipulated time.

Although most organizational guidelines differ from company to company, there are at least five ways of organizing internally to handle countertrade operations. First, the company has a countertrade coordinator without any staff, who is attached to purchasing, sales, the East European or other regional coordinating departments, or to a corporate staff office. Second, the company has a staff consultant for countertrade, who regularly advises all departments faced with countertrade obligations. Third, the company has a countertrade unit, comprising product, functional, and country specialists. Fourth, the company owns a share of an autonomous trading company, through which it disposes of countertrade obligations. Fifth, the company sets up an independent trading subsidiary or trading company. This may coordinate the countertrade activity of product divisions or dispose of countertrade obligations that cannot be absorbed and trade on its own account.

Because most large companies have already wrestled with countertrade problems, many executives find that one of these five variants already exists somewhere in their organizational structure. The challenge that faces executives in the 1980s is to determine which organizational form allows them the greatest freedom to increase earnings from an efficient countertrade policy. This chapter provides insights to help approach this issue in a positive fashion while avoiding costly pitfalls that can seriously damage countertrade operations.

A mid-1984 survey done by Business International of 130 companies engaged in countertrade clearly shows that a growing number of U.S. companies acknowledge that countertrade is not a temporary phenomenon. This is borne out by the surge in corporate interest in countertrade, as U.S. multinationals seek better ways to come to grips with the phenomenon. Of the 130 respondents that have engaged in countertrade activities, 37 companies (28 percent) have set up their own countertrade operations, of which 8 were full-fledged trading subsidiaries. Typically, the staffing of these units ran from two to four people but ranged up to eighteen full professionals in the case of Rockwell International Trading Company and forty-two in the case of Northrop.

The Business International survey illustrates just how the countertrade concept is spreading to different operations of multinationals. Almost half the companies that have organized themselves for countertrade have a marketing person to lead these responsibilities. This function is filled in a quarter of the cases by an executive with direct treasury or financial responsibility, indicating its importance in hedging financial risks or repatriating blocked funds. Executives with a purchasing background or responsibility, or with specific product expertise, accounted for 10 percent each in the category of key executives responsible for countertrade, the remainder being spread among such backgrounds as strategic planning, international business development, market research, and special projects.

CHOOSING AN ORGANIZATIONAL APPROACH

As noted earlier, the company has five alternative ways of organizing for countertrade: through the countertrade coordinator, the staff consultant, the corporate countertrade unit, shareholding in trading companies, and company-owned trading subsidiaries. Each of these options is examined in greater detail below. The first two alternatives are discussed together.

Countertrade Coordinator or Staff Consultant

Many companies already possess either a countertrade coordinator or maintain a staff consultant somewhere within their hierarchy. This is particularly true for firms that have faced countertrade in Eastern Europe but are now encountering countertrade pressure in other world markets.

Individuals may have been hired and given limited staff responsibility when the volume of countertrade was relatively low. Even where they performed with high efficiency, their record may be mixed. This is due to the fact that a large number of deals break down because of numerous factors beyond the control of an individual. Although the failure ratio is difficult to quantify, most countertrade experts consider a 5 percent success rate commendable. The transition to formation of a countertrade unit may be based on the conclusion that an individual staff member, regardless of effort, cannot effectively guide the countertrade policy for a large company.

Corporate Countertrade Units

Special corporate units for countertrade vary widely in size, function, and composition. The size of the staff depends on the volume of countertrade business they handle. One West German chemical group has a staff of fifty in its countertrade unit. Another European chemical company's unit is only half this size.

Successful operations cannot always be equated with a large countertrade unit. Many firms maintain such units with five or ten staff members and report a very effective management of countertrade obligations. A U.S. multinational that is noted for its countertrade skills has a special import arrangements department—that is, a countertrade unit—of six persons. The company reports that they are capable of buying everything from scrap metal to feathers around the globe.

Shareholding in Trading Companies

Numerous European trading companies have been founded by industrial companies, banks, and industrial groups. One key advantage is a relatively low cost per member company. Shareholders with marginal business that involves countertrade find that participation in a trading house allows them to dispose of occasional countertrade obligations in a reasonably effective manner. A jointly owned trading company may specialize in clearly defined goods if it is owned by a small number of shareholders with a limited product range.

But joint ownership can lead to conflicts of interest. The executives or staff of the trading company are accountable to several masters. There is little of the clear ownership relation that is obvious when one company establishes its own unit of trading subsidiary.

The jointly owned trading companies often complain that shareholders are usually not obliged to use their services. The shareholders often turn to them only in difficult cases. Frequently, the jointly owned company is asked to cope with cases in which the shareholder has accepted high counterpurchase obligations, agreed to severe penalties for nonfulfillment, and stated its final sales price without considering overhead costs or subsidy charges. The odds are good that the joint trading company will fail to settle the deal, irritating the shareholder who was originally responsible for the ill-advised countertrade commitment.

Some of the more successful jointly owned trading companies make it clear that they will not limit their business to the activity of their shareholders. They thus trade on their own account and accept countertrade obligations from nonshareholders.

Company-Owned Trading Subsidiaries

Among large multinationals the greatest current interest and concern is directed at the wholly owned independent trading subsidiary. In the Business International survey of U.S. companies involved in countertrade, of the thirty-seven corporations that have established a formal countertrade unit, eight chose to make a full-fledged trading subsidiary. A majority of the firms that have established such subsidiaries emphasized that it is risky to set up a very large, generalized trading company with sweeping, worldwide responsibilities. Successful trading companies usually begin much more modestly. An existing corporate countertrade unit may be separated from its staff position and chartered as a trading subsidiary. Or, a small trading company could be founded with a few specialists dealing in a limited range of products and markets.

There is no magical formula that indicates when companies should stop relying primarily upon independent trading houses and establish their own trading subsidiary. But companies reported that they began thinking seriously about such a move when they watched commission and subsidy payments to independent trading houses mount year after year with no apparent end in sight.

When does it pay to have your own trading unit? One corporate director offered an example of the arithmetic that could convince a company that a trading subsidiary had become necessary. A company might have countertrade obligations worth $4 million annually, for example. Assuming it paid subsidy charges averaging 10 percent to trading houses, it would cost the company $400,000 annually to have independent trading companies assume responsibility for disposal of the countertrade goods.

If the company established its own trading subsidiary, it certainly would *not* save $400,000 annually. It would still be required to offer attractive end-user discounts totaling, say, $200,000 to resell the countertrade goods. The savings could thus equal $200,000. If the salary and operating costs of several staff members and secretaries would be considerably below $200,000, then the company would be justified in establishing a small countertrade subsidiary.

Experienced corporate executives note that the time needed to create a successful operation from scratch will generally take one to two years.

Alternatively, it can be asked whether a company should acquire a trading house. Some executives have been dissatisfied with a cautious, slow-growth policy for a trading subsidiary. Their view could be characterized as follows: "If we need to trade, let us buy a trading house and start trading."

Superficially, this is an appealing alternative. It fits with the view still prevailing in some quarters that acquisitions are the best means of rapid corporate expansion. By buying an existing trading company a corporation can avoid years of drudgery in building up its own trading subsidiary, so the argument might run.

In reality, only a limited number of such acquisitions has occurred for one or more of the following reasons. One, nearly all successful trading houses operate a highly lucrative system of incentives and bonuses for their employees. The resultant income levels of senior staff are often far above the normal salary structure of Western multinationals. Two, effective countertrade specialists tend to be highly individualistic. It is doubtful whether an entire group of them could be integrated successfully into a large corporate structure. Three, when getting acquisition offers from multinational corporations, many owners of trading houses believe that this is the chance of a lifetime and demand exorbitant purchase prices. Four, an acquired trading subsidiary may not be easily reoriented toward serving corporate goals.

Such considerations do not mean that it is impossible to acquire a trading house successfully, but experience indicates this is a second-best solution.

CONSIDERATIONS IN ESTABLISHING A TRADING SUBSIDIARY

Assuming that a company has decided to opt for the establishment of a trading subsidiary, it has to consider the following: mission and charter statements, reporting channels, and relations to purchasing departments. Each of these considerations is discussed below.

Mission and Charter Statements

In normal business practice the establishment of any new unit is usually accompanied by a written charter or statement of mission on behalf of the parent company. Too frequently, executives told Business International in the survey, trading subsidiaries were founded with either a very vaguely worded charter statement or none at all.

For example, Alfa-Laval, a major Swedish agricultural equipment multinational, which in the past two years set up a trading subsidiary, spelled out in a very formal charter what the scope of the trading company's activities are to be. These include:

1. To fulfill Alfa-Laval's worldwide needs and commitments in the area of countertrade by: (a) concentrating the necessary expertise available throughout the organization; (b) supporting the group's sales force from the first negotiating phase until conclusion of the countertrade deal; and (c) handling all aspects of any countertrade commitment concluded.
2. To assist and act as liaison for all cooperation deals of Alfa-Laval companies that have a countertrade component.

3. To detect, monitor, and pursue general countertrade opportunities for Alfa-Laval's own projects and, if economically justified, to dispose of countertrade commitments for third parties.

4. To act as an agent for other multinationals the products or services of which do not compete with or otherwise conflict with Alfa-Laval's overall product and other interests. This extends to acting as an agent for state trading organizations in Eastern Europe and the LDCs in distributing their products and services worldwide.

A new trading company, by its very logic, will cut across established lines of authority within the corporation as it pursues its trading and countertrade business. Some executives will have their powers diminished. Other executives will profit from expanded opportunity. The potential for a disruptive turf fight or struggle for authority is a virtual certainty unless all involved parties clearly understand what the new trading company is supposed to do.

At the minimum, the charter statement must touch on several key issues including, for example, the following: Should the trading company be a profit center? What is its relationship with the corporation's product divisions? What financial controls will be exercised by corporate headquarters? What will be its obligation to handle countertrade or other units of the company? Will it be able to handle countertrade obligations of nonaffiliated parties?

Because the charter statement is a broad mandate, it does not normally deal with all technical points related to such issues. But it should at least provide a clear concept so that no executive can subsequently charge that the trading subsidiary has violated or failed to meet its mandate regarding trading and handling of countertrade.

Charter statements should also provide flexibility to cover future growth. As most trading companies are expected to start modestly in countertrade and in handling exports and imports before it can grow into more complex and generalized activities, the charter should be worded broadly enough to serve as an incentive to expanded activities.

Experienced executives noted to Business International an important tactical point: When a mission statement is being written, be sure that someone on the drafting team knows something about countertrade. They cited cases where the authors of a charter statement were staff officials who had had no experience with countertrade or, for that matter, no other general trading activities. Equally important, they stressed, the charter authors should have some idea of doing business with countries in which the company is facing or expects to face most of its countertrade problems.

Reporting Channels

A trading company can report to different parts of a parent corporation, depending on the purposes of the subsidiary and the scope of its responsibilities. It may report to the international division, a product division, a functional staff division, or directly to top management.

In a company with a separate international division the trading unit is likely to fall under the international division's jurisdiction. For example, the European trading subsidiary of a U.S. food-processing company reports to the director of international sales at U.S. headquarters.

Some trading subsidiaries were formed specifically to assist the needs of a product division. Consequently, they report to that division rather than the corporation as a whole. This may occur when the nature of the product forces one division to do a lot of trading while other divisions are able to sell their goods directly or concentrate on internal markets. Other subsidiaries are linked very closely with functional divisions. A growing number of U.S. companies see countertrade as essentially a financial exercise and, consequently, the trading subsidiary of such firms should report to the firms' financial authorities. This phenomenon goes hand in hand with the increased importance many multinationals ascribe to the treasury function as the global debt crisis makes trade financing, management of currency exposure, and the freeing up of blocked funds critical business issues.

In a few of the companies interviewed by Business International, the trading subsidiary reports to the company's top management. Such a direct reporting relationship ensures close supervision of the trading company but might also mean that it faces a more restricted role. This arrangement carries to the extreme the principle of "top-level support." But companies must be careful to ensure that corporate directors do not meddle in the day-to-day countertrade and trading transactions of the unit.

The choice of reporting channels is as much a result of functional considerations as it is one of taking into account the individual personalities of the managers filling a given position. Thus, what works for one company may not work in another.

Relations to Purchasing Departments

Some functions that trading subsidiaries perform for their parent corporations can overlap with functions performed by existing corporate divisions, particularly purchasing and export sales. A careful delineation of the functions of the trading company vis-à-vis other groups is essential to avoid overlapping responsibilities, duplication of efforts, and unhealthy competition between and among divisions. It is important to designate specific responsibilities of the trading company that are separate from those of the international purchasing and export sales functions.

In one variant the trading subsidiary may purchase specific goods and commodities for the various product divisions on a request basis. For example, a U.S. beverage manufacturer has a trading subsidiary that handles purchasing of countertrade goods, most of them related to the beverage industry. Occasionally, product divisions ask the trading subsidiary to look for particular types of countertrade goods that the divisions can use in their manufacturing process and will buy these goods from the trading company.

In some companies that have centralized purchasing departments the responsibilities are divided between the purchasing division and the trading company according to who is the final user of the purchased goods. The purchasing division does all the purchasing of goods used in-house, and the trading company buys only goods for resale outside the company. Eventually, if the trading company begins to play a greater role in the parent's import and export activities, it can take on responsibility for all purchasing, both for in-house use and sale to third parties.

PROFIT VERSUS COST CENTER

The point of greatest debate in the issue of trading units or subsidiaries is the question of whether it should be a profit center, or alternatively, a cost or service center. In response to the Business International survey of 130 companies involved in countertrade, 41 companies reported that their countertrade activities were organized as a profit center, and 57 were set up as cost centers to provide a service function. The remainder of the companies did not respond, primarily because their countertrade setup was not structured enough to make this question applicable. While the profit center setup tends to provide greater incentive for good performance, the cost or service center may be easier to push through in a company with many autonomous divisions headed by strong personalities. One executive who had experienced both modes of operation noted: "The only way we can get the other guys to cooperate is to change from a profit center to a cost center. We keep tab of our own performance and corporate management knows our worth."

There is no clear-cut solution to this problem. Both approaches contain inherent disadvantages, as well as positive features, which may be seized upon by executives favoring one particular organizational approach over another. Ultimately, top management must decide which way to pursue and issue clear organizational guidelines.

Most companies do not designate a new trading unit or subsidiary as a profit center right from the beginning, but allow the unit to expand gradually its activities and range of services. Once the trading unit or subsidiary develops a full range of skills and genuine earning potential, it may become a profit center.

Most of the trading subsidiaries interviewed by Business International were given between three and five years to become profitable—if it was intended at all to become a profit center. One trading subsidiary, for example, has been in existence for nearly five years, employs a staff of eighty people, and buys countertrade goods worth $270 million annually. Nevertheless, the unit still has not reached the profit stage, a fact that is acceptable within the context of overall corporate strategy.

Pros and Cons of Cost Centers

The cost center approach is the most conservative solution for handling countertrade commitments. Cost centers are primarily evaluated on the efficiency with which costs or budgets are controlled in providing services to other corporate divisions. The full benefits of their service accrue primarily to the product divisions for which they operate. Should the trading unit, however, be unable to find buyers for countertrade goods, the enormous amounts of energy wasted by its experts are often not appreciated, and all the blame for losing the deal is put on the countertrade unit.

Experienced executives emphasize that the intangible value of a nonprofit trading unit or subsidiary should not be overlooked. The competent settlement of countertrade obligations by a motivated service center staff is of greater value to the company's total sales performance than any heavy-handed calculation of the costs of a countertrade unit.

A countertrade unit may be able to find additional sales opportunities for the product divisions because staff members travel extensively in Eastern Europe and less developed countries and establish a wide range of business contacts. Although the value of these activities cannot be measured in dollars and cents, they can be very important to the entire company.

Managers of countertrade units are often called on to defend an activity that may never show a final bottom line profit. By way of defense, they keep a record of how many sales of the parent company to Eastern Europe or developing countries have been made possible with the help of their countertrade units.

The service center approach works well in cases in which the manager of the trading unit or subsidiary is highly loyal to the corporation and strives to support its objectives. Such persons are less likely to become involved in intracorporate squabbles or prestige fights to show the effectiveness of their own unit without relation to the needs of other divisions.

Reasons for Transforming Cost Centers into Profit Centers

Many executives maintain that the profit center approach reflects more accurately and visibly the benefits of the trading unit to the corporation. The trading unit or subsidiary will be much more motivated to fulfill its mission if profits are the basis for performance evaluation and rewards.

Cost centers usually are not evaluated according to the real market value of their services. The benefits are only enjoyed by the manufacturing divisions for which additional sales were made possible as the result of the countertrade unit's activities. Therefore, this form of organizational structure lacks motivation for cost center staff to work harder.

However, if a profit center knows that it will receive revenues from a division's sales, it will have a greater incentive to handle as many of the corporation's countertrade obligations as possible. The profit center approach works best when a strong entrepreneurial executive is put in charge. He or she will create new business opportunities, develop a wide range of contacts, train and retrain motivated staff, and try to expand earnings in an aggressive way to show the subsidiary in the best possible light.

Should Subsidiaries be Allowed to Work for Third Parties?

One of the most controversial questions in establishing a countertrade organization is whether the trading subsidiary should be given the right to work for third parties. Good trading executives are entrepreneurs who show initiative to seek out new business opportunities. Consequently, there is a tendency for the trading subsidiary to expand its operations and seek to work for third parties. However, some parent corporations resist this growth, feeling that it may take away from the primary function of the trading subsidiary, that being to promote sales of the parent company. They may write into the charter statement severe limitations on the freedom of the trading company to work for other parties.

Executives of several trading subsidiaries complained to Business International that their units, although in operation for more than three or four years, still do not make any profits, in part because their activity is restricted to the settlement of the parent company's countertrade obligations. A number of trading units or subsidiaries must restrict their purchases to products that can be used in-house or, at most, may buy only related products for resale. They are not permitted to buy unrelated goods even if they believe that they could dispose of such products without a loss.

The majority of trading subsidiaries interviewed by Business International believe that a countertrade operation can become profitable only if it is allowed to work for third parties. There are several reasons listed for such an assumption. One, the compensation received from the parent company, regardless of whether it is a fee, commission, or percentage of sale price, is never enough to make the operation profitable. Two, if the countertrade unit gets the right to work for third parties, it can achieve profits from such deals which can make up for the losses incurred in settling the parent's countertrade obligations. Three, through their many contacts both in the socialist and capitalist countries, the traders find new business opportunities, new suppliers and buyers. Many opportunities are lost because charters forbid work for outsiders. Four, countertrade obligations of the parent may fluctuate so much that the subsidiary is overworked at one stage and underemployed in another. Therefore, any free time should be allotted for deals with outside parties. Five, sometimes trading subsidiaries are offered bigger lots than they need for in-house use by their parents. In such cases, the right to deal with third parties is a must.

However, the right to work for third parties also involves some problems. As such deals usually are more profitable, there is a tendency to prefer business with outside firms and neglect countertrade commitments of the parent company. Some executives of parent companies told Business International that their trading subsidiaries continually discovered or invented excuses that prevented them from working for their parents. The subsidiaries had found that third-party deals were so much more lucrative that they did not want to waste time servicing their own corporations.

In one case a trading subsidiary was told that it must make a net profit of at least 3 percent on any deal. The unit agreed on the condition that they could treat the parent just like any other client. As a result, deals with third parties were preferred whenever they offered a higher profitability. In another extreme instance the trading company would not even discuss basic countertrade pitfalls with newly assigned executives in the corporate marketing divisions because it was "too busy" with third-party transactions.

In order to avoid such extremes, a number of firms have granted their subsidiaries the right to engage in third-party deals. At the same time, they drafted the charter statement so that assignments from the parent firm enjoy absolute priority over work for third parties. Moreover, all countertrade obligations of individual product divisions must be fulfilled, ahead of third-party commitments.

HOW TO ALLOCATE COSTS AND REVENUES

Besides debating the merits and limitations associated with a profit- versus cost-center approach, the company has to consider the issues of cost assessment and revenue policy. Each of these considerations is discussed below.

Assessing Costs

In evaluating the performance of a trading operation, it is important to measure accurately the costs that are attributable to the unit. This is easy for all direct costs, such as salaries, travel, and office supplies. But indirect or hidden costs are subject to allocation by management, such as services rendered to the trading unit or subsidiary by legal, accounting, or finance departments in the company's headquarters.

Quantifying such costs can be tricky and complicated. Companies can use a number of ways in allocating indirect costs, including the following: One, the trading unit or subsidiary may pay only a token sum to the parent company for the use of support services. Two, some companies insist on more than token payment and bill their units or subsidiaries costs as they occur. Three, the unit or subsidiary pays a fixed monthly or annual fee based on estimates of actual costs.

Revenue Policy

The earnings of trading units or subsidiaries may or may not include compensation by their parent for the counterpurchase services provided. This depends on whether the trading outfit is treated as a cost or a profit center. Companies use various methods of compensating trading units for their assistance in fulfilling counterpurchase obligations. (The percentage in parentheses indicates the share of Business International questionnaire respondents that indicated a particular form as the dominant revenue source.)

No Compensation. Trading units working as a cost center frequently do not get any compensation at all for their efforts. They have to get rid of the countertrade goods at the best possible price. Losses from the sale of countertrade goods are deducted from the profits of the product sales division. The unit just has to control its expenses to stay within budget (17 percent).

Fees Based on Time Allocation. If a trading unit works for several manufacturing divisions, it may charge the individual product groups based on the estimated time required to handle specific countertrade commitments. This helps to determine which division is using the countertrade unit most (7 percent).

Charging a Fixed Percentage of the Sales Price or Countertrade Commitment. In many companies product divisions pay a certain percentage of the sales price to the countertrade unit if and when the unit facilitates an export involving countertrade. Other trading units receive a fixed percentage based on the value of the countertrade commitment. The percentage rates are fixed in advance and do not vary from case to case. Selling units of the company prefer this arrangement because it makes price calculations much easier. A certain fixed percentage is incorporated in the sales price to cover the countertrade obligation, and no callbacks are necessary in each individual case to find out from countertrade experts how much has to be added to the price if countertrade is involved. However, this method does not distinguish between difficult countertrade obligations and countertrade goods that are easy to dispose of. It overlooks the varying discounts that have to be paid to the end-users who ultimately buy the countertrade goods. Moreover, the countertrade unit is expected to compensate those deals where it suffers losses with others where it makes a profit. As a result, many countertrade units working under such a system are inclined to handle only easy deals that are profitable. If possible, they refuse under various pretexts to handle unprofitable and difficult assignments, thus defeating the basic goal of helping the company handle its countertrade obligations (14 percent).

Charging Varying Handling Fees. This is the method most commonly used by multinational corporations to calculate the revenues of their trading units or subsidiaries. This method is best suited to reflect the varying degrees of effort necessary to fulfill countertrade commitments. Should a countertrade unit be able to resell countertrade goods without any loss, the handling fees may be as low as 1 percent. However, if the goods have to be resold at a large discount, the fee is much higher. In a number of cases, companies set a maximum fee that can be charged by the countertrade unit—for example, 10 to 15 percent of the countertrade obligation. At the beginning of the negotiations company salespeople quote to their customers a price that incorporates this maximum fee. Should the countertrade unit indicate that it will require only a lower handling fee for the disposal of the countertrade goods, the salespeople can still grant a discount to the potential buyers (37 percent).

Charging Normal Commission Rates. Trading units or subsidiaries that are in a strong position may be able to charge product divisions the same commissions and subsidies that independent trading houses would ask for providing the same services. In a number of cases, the countertrade unit is required to calculate average commission rates quoted by three independent trading houses. As a rule, manufacturing divisions must use their own trading unit or subsidiary, even if outside dealers might be willing to work for a lower fee. The reason behind this policy is that the company-owned trading group should earn the profit which otherwise would go to outside trading houses. However, such an arrangement may lead to frictions with product divisions, which often claim that their profits are so low that every percentage point saved in commissions and subsidies may be decisive for the profitability of a sale (25 percent).

In the above remarks, we have recapitulated certain key issues in the development of U.S. trading activities. We have looked at the reasons why companies are establishing trading subsidiaries, reviewed the organizational implications of such subsidiaries, discussed the charter statement, and considered the effects of cost versus profit center status.

These trading activities are new and their future course of development is impossible to chart with certainty. They are surely not *sogo shosha*, and they may or may not come to resemble the *sogo shosha* for a long time. Time and experience—as well as a commitment to trading as a legitimate function of a company—are the essential elements for success in this field. U.S. companies are at least beginning to move in the right direction.

STRATEGIC MANAGEMENT IN THE MANUFACTURING SECTOR

8 STRATEGIC MANAGEMENT IN MANUFACTURING
The Case of Aircrafts

Thomas J. Bacher

Let me first briefly introduce Boeing. Our annual sales are about $10 billion, more than half of which come from commercial aircraft, with the balance from the military and space sectors.

Contrary to popular opinion, the commercial aircraft business is fiercely independent and competitive. We received less than 1 percent of the cost of funding R&D programs from government subsidies. The remainder comes from our own investment and capital, and at our own risk. Airbus, on the other hand, receives large subsidies from the sponsoring governments. They have lost an estimated $10 to $12 billion to date (1984 dollars), the level within this range depending upon whether real interest cost (at about 3 percent) is included. With the addition of the A320 program, the Airbus loss will grow to about $18 billion by 1995, including real interest cost. So you can see the kind of competition that we are facing in this contest between state capitalism and private capitalism. In addition to the European subsidy issue, other competitive imbalances imposed on U.S. producers include export controls, antibribery regulations, and extraterritorial application of U.S. laws.

Boeing's commercial airplane business is about 60 percent foreign. Therefore, we are very much dependent on foreign sales. About 24 percent or roughly one-quarter of our sales are dependent on foreign procurement. That is, many countries demand subcontract or offset work as a condition of sales. These countries want a "piece of the industrial action." It is not usually so much countertrade that the countries involved want but rather to build part of the airplane. These demands come from industrialized countries with established aircraft manufacturing industries as well as from developing countries that are anxious to develop new industrial capabilities.

Commercial aircraft production is a complicated industry. It is a low-volume industry with about 280 units currently in annual production. Commercial aircraft production has been as high as 740 units in a single year. It takes about $1.5 to $2 billion in developmental costs to launch a new commercial transport program. The total cash flow investment can typically be double this amount. It takes fifteen to twenty years to recover this investment and break even, if breakeven is achieved at all.

Turning our attention now to Japan, the Japanese aerospace industry, both military and commercial, is relatively small. In terms of our cooperation with them, we have sold about 164 airplanes (all models included) to Japan, the combined worth of which is almost $10 billion, or equivalent to about one million cars. To state it another way, if they sell us a million cars, we are just about even in terms of trade balance. To put it into perspective, all of Japan's airlines—All Nippon, Japan Airlines, Tao Domestic, Southwest Airlines, and Nippon Cargo Airlines—together have about 200 commercial airplanes in service, whereas United Airlines alone has 400.

Boeing's cooperation with Japanese industrial firms dated back to early 1969, when Mitsubishi Heavy Industries did subcontracting work for our 747. This was followed by subcontract work to other major Japanese aerospace producers, namely Kawasaki Heavy Industries and Fuji Heavy Industries. Boeing's discussions with Civil Transport Development Corporation (CTDC)—a quasi-government Japanese entity that serves as the focal point for cooperative discussions involving Japanese aerospace firms—began in the early 1970s. This led to Japanese participation on the Boeing 767, beginning in 1978. Currently, we are talking with the representatives of the Japanese aerospace industry through the Japan Aircraft Development Corporation (JADC) about collaboration on a possible new model, frequently designated by Boeing as the 7-7 and by the Japanese as the YXX. Japan also manufactures equipment items for Boeing. They have a helicopter licensing agreement.

With regard to the 767, body sections and wing panels are manufactured in Japan. They are under contract to the CTDC, which is the coordinative focal point for such work actually produced by Mitsubishi Heavy Industries, Kawasaki Heavy Industries, and Fuji Heavy Industries. Japanese participation in the 767 program represents about 7.5 percent of total program costs, or about 15 percent of the airframe work, the airframe work constituting half of the total program cost. So it is not a particularly large share. It is a growing relationship, however. The 767 is not a joint venture and Japan is not involved on an equity basis. We call Japan a program participant. It is really a form of risk-sharing subcontracting. (See Tung 1984: ch. 5.)

In the current 7-7/YXX collaborative discussions between Japan and Boeing, the arrangement under consideration would be a true joint program involving equity participation by Japan. However, we have not as yet determined the precise nature or name of the legal entity under such an arrangement.

Why do we collaborate with the Japanese? One reason is that we are a market-oriented organization. Japanese participation would not ensure sales but would ensure that Boeing products would enjoy a fair opportunity to compete in that market, and if all other factors are equal, would likely enjoy a competitive edge. This is what we call improved market access. A second reason is risk and investment sharing; the Japanese would share in this regard at least proportionate to equity position. This leads us to the third reason for collaboration: improved profitability to Boeing. A major hangup with Japan and other potential partners has to do with what the Japanese call *norandi*. This is some form of payment that we expect other partners to pay to Boeing since they offer less in terms of overall experience, expertise, and capabilities which enhance prospects for potential success of the program. Boeing has insisted on a provision called "weighted-revenue sharing." Under this provision Boeing would receive a share of program revenues that is proportionately larger than its equity position. A fourth reason for collaboration is improved sales and export-financing support. Partners would provide access to the export-financing banks or the appropriate agencies of their governments (i.e., their equivalent to our Export-Import Bank).

The status of our collaborative discussions with JADC is covered in a letter of understanding that indicates the desire of the parties to collaborate on a future new program (7-7/YXX), in which Japan would have a 25 percent equity position and Boeing would retain a minimum of 51 percent. The balance would go to other prospective participants or to Boeing. Under this concept JADC would contribute approximately 25 percent of the effort and investment required of such a program. Furthermore, the Japanese firms would enjoy broad functional involvement. They would not be limited to manufacturing and operational functions but would also be involved in design engineering, sales, marketing, product support, and so on. All the costs of the venture would be based on Boeing (U.S.) costs and productivity standards and would be quoted in U.S. dollars. The Japanese would therefore also assume a currency or foreign exchange rate risk. All parties would assume cost performance risk. If they underrun allowable costs, they would retain the resulting financial benefits. Conversely, cost overruns would be borne by the parties responsible for such performance. Boeing will not compromise the price of the product by virtue of foreign participation.

A number of important issues come to mind with regard to international collaboration between the United States and Japan. What are the potential advantages? How do such advantages balance out against the risk of helping to establish a future competitor? What is the Japanese approach to the industry? What are the essential industry characteristics of past successes by Japanese industry, and how does that pattern relate to the commercial aircraft industry? What is the likelihood that Japan will become an independent competitor in commercial aircraft? What is the potential impact on U.S. jobs?

In order to respond to these questions it is helpful first to describe the characteristics of the aircraft industry. It is a low-volume production industry. Unlike the automobile industry, in which 30 million cars are produced worldwide each year, total world commercial aircraft production averages only 300 units per year. Because it is a low-volume but highly competitive industry, the financial consequences for all but the most successful programs can be very severe. To illustrate, the interest alone on just the $2 billion development cost for a new program is about $200 million a year. So, if you produce 20 airplanes per year, the interest cost alone is $10 million per copy. This low-volume characteristic of the industry limits the number of prime contractors that it can economically support. If a company does not produce 500 airplanes during the first ten years of delivery, it will lose its proverbial shirt. It is a high-risk, high-cost, highly volatile, and very cyclical industry. Two to three years ago Boeing went from producing thirty-two airplanes a month to the current level of twelve to fourteen. We are moving back to the sixteen to eighteen monthly level, reflecting a 50 percent variation in a three-year cycle. This variation is much larger than that of the automotive and other industries that seem to feel they have political and social problems. The average breakeven period is twelve to fifteen years from program start. With regard to employment, Boeing went from 150,000 people in 1968 to 50,000 in 1972. Recently, we laid off 25,000 people out of 100,000 in a three-year cycle. Then there is also a large technical risk; one serious failure can put a company out of business. The Comet illustrates the type of technical risks that can be encountered.

What is the targeted industry approach in Japan? Figure 8-1 illustrates my conception of the way the Ministry of International Trade and Industry (MITI) and other government agencies primarily promote, encourage, and subsidize an industry. They import technology by any and all means available. They control the domestic competition through multicompany cooperation. That combination of strategies develops the industry capability. They control the competition and thereby increase domestic consumption, which in turn raises production volume and reduces costs. When they have achieved this capability they are then able to enter the international market as a low-cost competitor. The United States has not targeted at all in a governmental sense along these lines.

Now, if you take that targeting approach and apply it to commercial aircraft, it reveals certain incompatibilities.

Figure 8-2 illustrates the criteria or requirements to make Japan's targeted industry approach work. A first requirement is a large domestic market. In Japan's case, the domestic market for commercial aircraft is very small. They represent about 5 percent of the world market, and that is not big enough to support a large production volume. Consequently, they cannot first build an industry through a protected home market. A second requirement is the potential for large-volume production. As I indicated earlier, the aircraft industry is typified by low-volume production. A third requirement is significant potential for innovations to the production process. The potential for this in the aircraft industry is somewhat limited due to restricted volume and the cyclical nature of the industry. A fourth requirement is orientation toward technology exploitation rather than technology development. The Japanese fare reasonably well on this criterion since they are oriented toward both. A fifth requirement is limited market risk and low volatility. This criterion is not met, as discussed earlier. A sixth requirement is employment

STRATEGIC MANAGEMENT IN MANUFACTURING

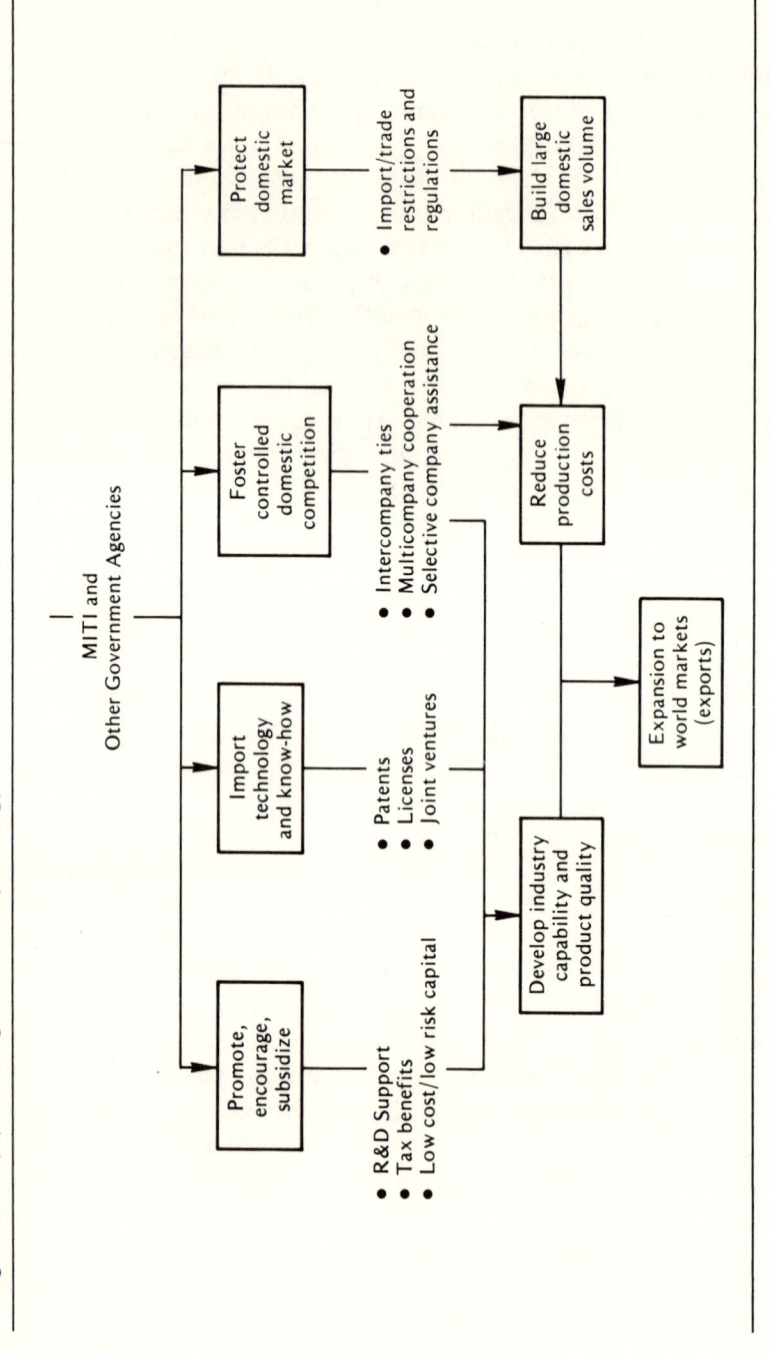

Figure 8-1. Japan's Targeted Industry Strategy.

Figure 8-2. Japanese Requirements for Success versus Commercial Aircraft Industry Characteristics.

Japanese Requirement	Reality	Compatibility Rating
Large domestic market	Small domestic market	x
Large-volume production potential	Low-volume production	x
Significant potential for innovations to production process	Moderate potential	o
Oriented toward technology exploitation, rather than development	Oriented toward both	o
Limited market risk and volatility	Highly volatile market and related risk	x
Employment stability	Large swings in employment	x
Related military market base not essential	Important	o
Adequate resources for multiproduct capability (intermediate term)	Inadequate resources for significant time period	x

Rating: ● Excellent;   o Good/fair;   X Deficient.

stability. The lifetime employment practice of Japan does not fit the large swings in employment characteristic of the industry. A seventh requirement is a related military market base. This is important in Japan; hence there is a good/fair fit here. An eighth requirement is adequate resources for multiproduct capability. At present Japan does not have the aerospace capability to produce a family of commercial aircraft models. The combined aerospace employment of the major Japanese aerospace firms that are potential producers of commercial aircraft is about one-tenth that of Boeing. Therefore, it will be some time before this criterion can be satisfied.

The preceding rationale explains why we are willing to take the risk of collaborating with Japan—because commercial aircraft does not fit the pattern of their targeted industry approach. It is a very different type of business from those in Japan that achieved preeminence through the targeted industry approach described earlier. They recognize their limited capability, the tremendous investment and risk, and the highly competitive environment. Although their government helps in the financial development, Japanese private industry must assume the risk of producing and marketing. This differs from Europe, where the government subsidizes all phases of the industry. On the Boeing 767 joint program, for example, the participating firms under the umbrella of CTDC have already paid back two-thirds of the government investment. So MITI agrees with us, you might say, on our evaluation of their potential competitiveness in the future. Hence, they have decided that they want cooperation instead of competition.

Figure 8–3 illustrates how the aircraft industry is somewhat unique among the targeted industries, both past and present. The Japanese aircraft sector is deficient in many of the factors or requirements to make it a successful targeted industry.

Figure 8–4 further illustrates the difference between the commercial aircraft industry and other industries in Japan that have been highly successful. It depicts what I call their start-up years. The bars represent the percentage of Japanese production for local, indigenous consumption during these early years. Note that more than 50 percent, sometimes as high as 60 to 80 percent, of production for the industries shown went for indigenous consumption. In 1982 one-half of their automotive output was for Japanese consumption. In the case of crude steel, it was as high as 70 percent. In computers 70 percent was for the domestic market. Even with wristwatches

THE CASE OF AIRCRAFTS 95

Figure 8-3. How the Aircraft Industry Differs From Other Targeted Industries.

Japanese Industrial Success-Compatibility Factors	Past Successes									New Targets						
	Steel	Shipbuilding	Machine tools	Motor vehicles	Radios, TVs	Watches	Cameras	Aircraft	Computers	Fiber optics	Biotechnology	Robotics	Composites—carbon fiber	Integrated circuits—semiconductors
Large domestic market	●	●	●	●	●	●	●	×	●	●	●	●	●	●
Potential for high-volume production	●	●	●	●	●	●	●	×	●	●	●	●	●	●
Significant potential for innovations to production process	●	●	●	●	●	●	●	○	●	●	●	○	●	●
Oriented toward technology exploitation, rather than develop	●	●	●	●	●	●	●	○	○	○	×	○	○	○
Limited market risk and volatility	●	●	●	●	●	●	●	×	●	●	●	●	●	●
Employment stability	●	●	●	●	●	●	●	×	●	●	●	●	●	●
Related military market base not essential	●	○	●	●	●	●	●	○	●	●	●	●	●	●
Resources for multiple product capability	●	●	●	●	●	●	●	×	●	●	●	●	●	●

Rating: ● Excellent; ○ Good; × Deficient.

96   STRATEGIC MANAGEMENT IN MANUFACTURING

Figure 8-4. Percentage of Sales from the Japanese Domestic Market, High-Export Products.

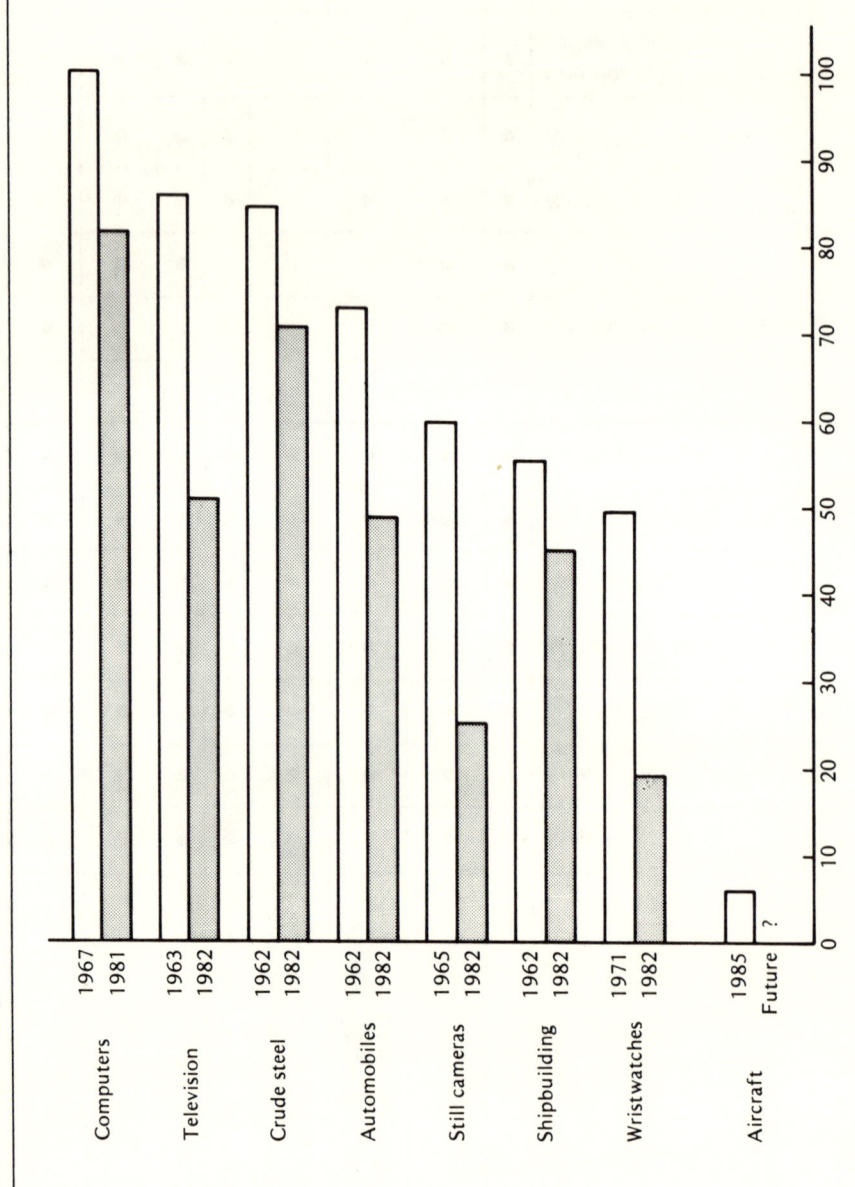

and cameras, one-fourth to one-fifth of production was for local consumption.

As previously mentioned, Japan's market for commercial aircraft represents only 5 percent of the world market and is simply not large enough to justify the past Japanese approach. We believe these considerations explain why Japan is committed to a collaborative approach in commercial aircraft. Boeing believes that it can benefit from such an arrangement and that it preempts the possibility of Japanese collaboration with a competitor.

Properly structured, we believe that Boeing/Japan cooperation can also be very beneficial to the United States. Our studies show that the loss of U.S. jobs by virtue of Japanese participation would be more than offset by increased sales volume resulting from such participation. In addition to a net jobs benefit for the United States, successful international sales translate into trade balance benefits. Japan represents the largest foreign market for commercial aircraft; continued access to that market is therefore extremely important to both Boeing and the United States.

REFERENCES

Tung, R.L. 1984. *Business Negotiations with the Japanese.* Lexington, Mass.: LexingtonBooks, D.C. Heath.

9 STRATEGIC MANAGEMENT IN MANUFACTURING
The Case of Pharmaceuticals

Leonard Wimpfheimer

The size of the free world market for pharmaceuticals is about $72 billion, Japan alone accounting for 18 percent of it or about $13 billion (ex manufacturer). The importance of Japan is even more dramatic when you view the foreign market in isolation. Japan dominates the total overseas market and represents more than one-third of it. The U.S. market is about half the size of the total free world market, the balance being the overseas or free foreign markets.

These figures are somewhat misleading because the Japanese pharmaceutical sector is even more dominant in certain therapeutic categories. In antibiotics, for example, Japan represents by far the largest single market in the world. It represents more than half of the total export anitbiotic market and is even larger than the United States anitbiotic sector. Antibiotics are a $2.5 billion business in Japan. Antibiotics are administered either orally or intravenously. The oral and intravenous sectors are roughly equal in terms of percentages. These statistics suggest that a multinational company in the pharmaceutical industry, particularly in the antibiotic sector, must be present in Japan.

When we talk about the leading international pharmaceutical products of the world, Japanese companies are not as prominent as one might expect. For example, excluding the United States, there are only ten pharmaceutical products with sales exceeding $100 million on an international basis. Of these, three are Japanese, one of which is limited to sales in Japan. This is Futraful, which is an anticancer drug.

The Japanese are now placing an increasing emphasis on their research and development. Japanese pharmaceutical companies now spend anywhere from 7 to 10 percent of corporate sales on research and development. This was not the case a number of years ago. The Japanese have an economic advantage over their U.S. counterparts in the development of new drugs. For example, it costs the Japanese companies approximately $35 to $50 million to develop a new drug, whereas it costs Merck approximately $70 million. We believe that Japanese development costs will increase gradually as they market more of their products overseas, thus requiring drug approval and registration in numerous countries. Whether this economic advantage that the Japanese have in developing new drugs will continue is unknown; it will depend largely on whether there is reciprocity between the U.S. and Japanese governmental regulatory agencies in accepting foreign clinical and safety data.

CHARACTERISTICS OF THE JAPANESE PHARMACEUTICAL MARKET

Japan plays a major role in world pharmaceuticals. In 1960–1980 it ranked fourth in the development of new drugs in the free world market. By 1981 they had fifteen of the sixty-five patented new products. In 1982 the United States and Japan were tied for first place, each with nine out of thirty-nine patented drugs. In 1983 the Japanese became number one with ten out of forty patented products. These numbers can be misleading since a new drug is not always a Tagamet-type blockbuster. New drugs may be modified or reformulated drugs that are not breakthroughs in a given therapeutic class.

Besides the importance of the Japanese international market, there are a number of points about the Japanese pharmaceutical market that are especially noteworthy. One of these is the rigid safety clinical requirements of the Japanese regulatory agency, *Koseisho*. A couple of years ago *Koseisho* barely opened its doors to U.S. data. Even now they will accept U.S. clinical data only if the tests were performed with Japanese subjects living in the United States. The limited number of Japanese citizens living in the United States and their unavailability for tests reduce this regulation to virtually "no change" in actual practice.

However, Japan now accepts foreign stability data and animal study data. I think we are slowly going to see regulatory reciprocity. The Japanese will probably accept more of our data and the United States will accept more of theirs. The United States would probably be pleased to work out a reciprocal arrangement. Good medical practices are becoming more standardized not only in Japan but around the world. If a good antiulcer drug or good antihypertensive drug is developed in Japan, it will be considered a good antiulcer or antihypertensive drug in the United States, Europe, and around the world.

Presently, there are over 1,200 manufacturers of pharmaceuticals in Japan, about 400 of which can be considered major. However, no single indigenous or foreign company has more than a 7 percent share of the total pharmaceutical market in Japan. In contrast, it is not uncommon for a leading pharmaceutical company in the United States, West Germany, or Australia to have over a 10 percent market share. There will probably be a consolidation of the Japanese pharmaceutical industry and it will increasingly resemble that of the other major markets in the world, in terms of dominance by ten to twenty major companies.

I will discuss some characteristics of the Japanese pharmaceutical industry that are relevant from the strategic management standpoint.

One, the Japanese are probably the most health-conscious people in the world. Virtually every Japanese businessman carries a small kit of pharmaceuticals when he travels. I do not know how many Americans do this, but I believe the practice is far from universal.

Two, Japan is the second-largest pharmaceutical market in the world (behind the United States), representing a higher per capita consumption of pharmaceuticals than any other market in the world.

Three, the government appears to encourage R&D-oriented companies through the health scheme that is explained later. In Japan the *Koseisho*, which is equivalent to our Food and Drug Administration (FDA), approves drugs just as the FDA does here. After approval *Koseisho* grants a National Health Scheme (NHI) price which is the regulated patient price. The physician charges the patient this price for prescription drugs, but the patient is reimbursed for virtually the entire price. This selling price is revised downward every year or two, never upward. A pharmaceutical company cannot increase the price even if costs go up. In the past several years there have been drastic reductions in the NHI or consumer prices of pharmaceuticals. In 1981, 1983, and 1984 the *Koseisho* reduced NHI prices. This downward revision of prices of existing drugs encourages the development of new drugs because a company can usually get a premium for them. The government encourages more R&D to develop superior pharmaceuticals which can reduce the length of hospital stays and thus cut down overall health care costs. In this manner the Japanese government either directly or indirectly encourages the development of new drugs. For this reason, a number of small generic manufacturers of "me-too" drugs have become unprofitable.

Four, Japan is a highly ethical, scientifically oriented country where medicine is practiced much as it is in the United States. Japanese doctors are extremely well informed. In fact, the Japanese are second only to the British in terms of being well read. This becomes evident when one visits a Japanese physician's office and sees the astonishing number of Japanese and foreign medical journals that are piled on his or her desk. Many Japanese doctors will follow the trend or be influenced by leading international physicians' publications. In addition, there is a distinct medical advantage for a Japanese doctor to prescribe a more expensive drug. It is often to a patient's advantage to get a more advanced and efficacious medication which can speed up his or her recovery. Since patients are fully reimbursed for these expenses, there is no incentive for them not to use a new drug.

Five, the Japanese pharmaceutical companies are on a par with advanced multinational companies in the rest of the world in terms of their sales turnover, research expenditure, type of products marketed, and so on. These companies have a potential to become worldwide marketers and tough competitors around the world.

Six, Japan will have to relax its requirements for data from foreign countries in the future. This may be considered a form of reciprocity. If Japan does this, the U.S. and European regulatory agencies may be more tolerant in accepting Japanese data. Since Japanese pharmaceutical companies have already spent huge sums in developing new drugs for their home market, they will be forced to expand into new markets, such as the United States, to maximize the return on their investment. We can surely expect to see more Japanese pharmaceuticals in the United States in the future.

There are a number of negative aspects about the Japanese pharmaceutical industry. First, the NHI or consumer price always goes down. There was an 18 percent average price decrease in 1981, a 5 percent cut in 1983, a 16.5 percent reduction in 1984, and another decrease in March 1985. If these were compounded, it represents an approximate average decrease of 35 percent in the NHI price of drugs over a three-year period. This was even more dramatic for certain drugs which were reduced as much as 40 percent. Hence, for many manufacturers of generic drugs and small companies, it is very difficult to operate in the Japanese pharmaceutical market.

Second, the complex distribution system discourages the entry of foreign companies. Many of the Japanese companies that distribute pharmaceuticals in the country have special relationships with a wholesaler, so that the latter will promote the former's products. In some cases, large Japanese pharmaceutical companies have certain equity ownership of their wholesalers. It is often difficult to know exactly what the relationship is. It is virtually impossible for a U.S. or European company to work in Japan without being "plugged into" some existing network of distribution. Effective sales distribution is a key to success in Japan.

Third, the strict regulatory requirements mandate that clinical trials be done in Japan on Japanese subjects, which is often expensive for foreign companies. It means setting up a laboratory in Japan and hiring technical people in Japan to generate the required regulatory data.

Fourth, the large number of detail calls by sales representatives on physicians necessitates a very large sales force. In Japan a sales representative makes more frequent calls on a doctor as compared to the United States or Europe. In the United States it is usual to call on a physician once every one to three months, depending on whether the physician is a specialist in a hospital or a general practitioner. The Japanese sales representative, on the other hand, typically calls on a physician as often as once or twice a week. If a foreign company does not follow this practice, the Japanese physicians may interpret it as a lack of interest on the part of the company.

As in the case of other countries, the Japanese government is trying to reduce its health care cost. To prevent many of the government-subsidized programs from operating at a loss, the Japanese government had proposed that patients start paying 10 percent of their medical costs in 1984. Subsequently, this was to increase to

20 percent. As of summer of 1985 this proposal has been delayed, as it has become a major political issue. However, it is generally believed that this measure will be implemented.

Another aspect of health care cost containment is that the government appears to force pharmaceutical companies to become more research oriented. In order to survive the ongoing NHI price reductions, companies have to generate new and more effective drugs which will in turn cut down on hospitalization and overall health care expenses.

The Japanese companies have become more R&D conscious and plan to internationalize. The urgency for Japanese pharmaceutical companies to internationalize stems from the need to recover the heavy expenditures they have been making in research and development. The Japanese pharmaceutical manufacturers have developed a huge research base and now they must recover their costs and generate a satisfactory return on investment. With all the new drugs coming out, the Japanese pharmaceutical companies have to expand overseas since the Japanese market is not large enough to accommodate all these new drugs on a profitable basis. Figure 9-1 shows the ten leading pharmaceutical corporations in the world. Note that no Japanese companies rank among those listed. Shionogi and Takeda rank among the top fifteen pharmaceutical companies in the world in terms of sales turnover, but they are not considered to be multinational.

Despite this existing structure, the leading Japanese pharmaceutical manufacturers are poised to become leading multinational factors. If we look at the leading Japanese companies, such as Shionogi, Takeda, Sankyo, Fujisawa, Eisai, Green Cross, and Yamanouchi, we can see an emerging overseas presence. The top companies in Japan are generally in the $500 to $750 million category for pharmaceutical sales, which is comparable to the sales of the largest U.S. companies in this country. Admittedly, the leading U.S., German, and Swiss multinationals are in the $1 to $2 billion category, but this represents their worldwide sales, not a single market. In contrast, most of the sales of Japanese pharmaceutical companies are generated within Japan.

The leading Japanese companies now spend about 10 percent of their pharmaceutical sales on research. This can be a bit confusing since most of the Japanese manufacturers also sell other products, and the percentage of total research expenditures often appears to

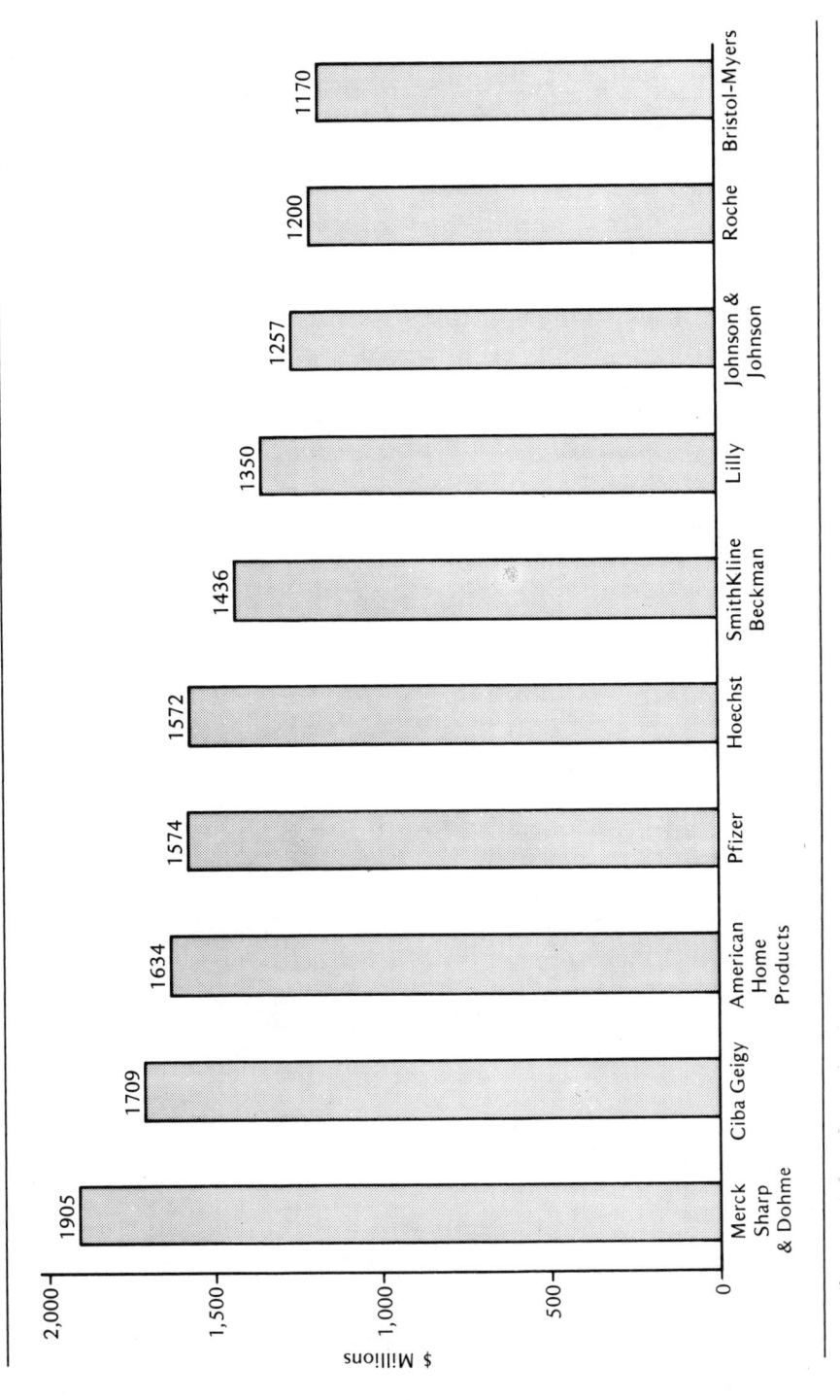

Figure 9-1. Leading Corporations, World Market, 1983.

Company	$ Millions
Merck Sharp & Dohme	1905
Ciba Geigy	1709
American Home Products	1634
Pfizer	1574
Hoechst	1572
SmithKline Beckman	1436
Lilly	1350
Johnson & Johnson	1257
Roche	1200
Bristol-Myers	1170

Source: IMS International, Inc., Zug, Switzerland, 1984.

Figure 9-2. Japanese Pharmaceutical Market—Market Share versus Number of *Propa*, 1983.

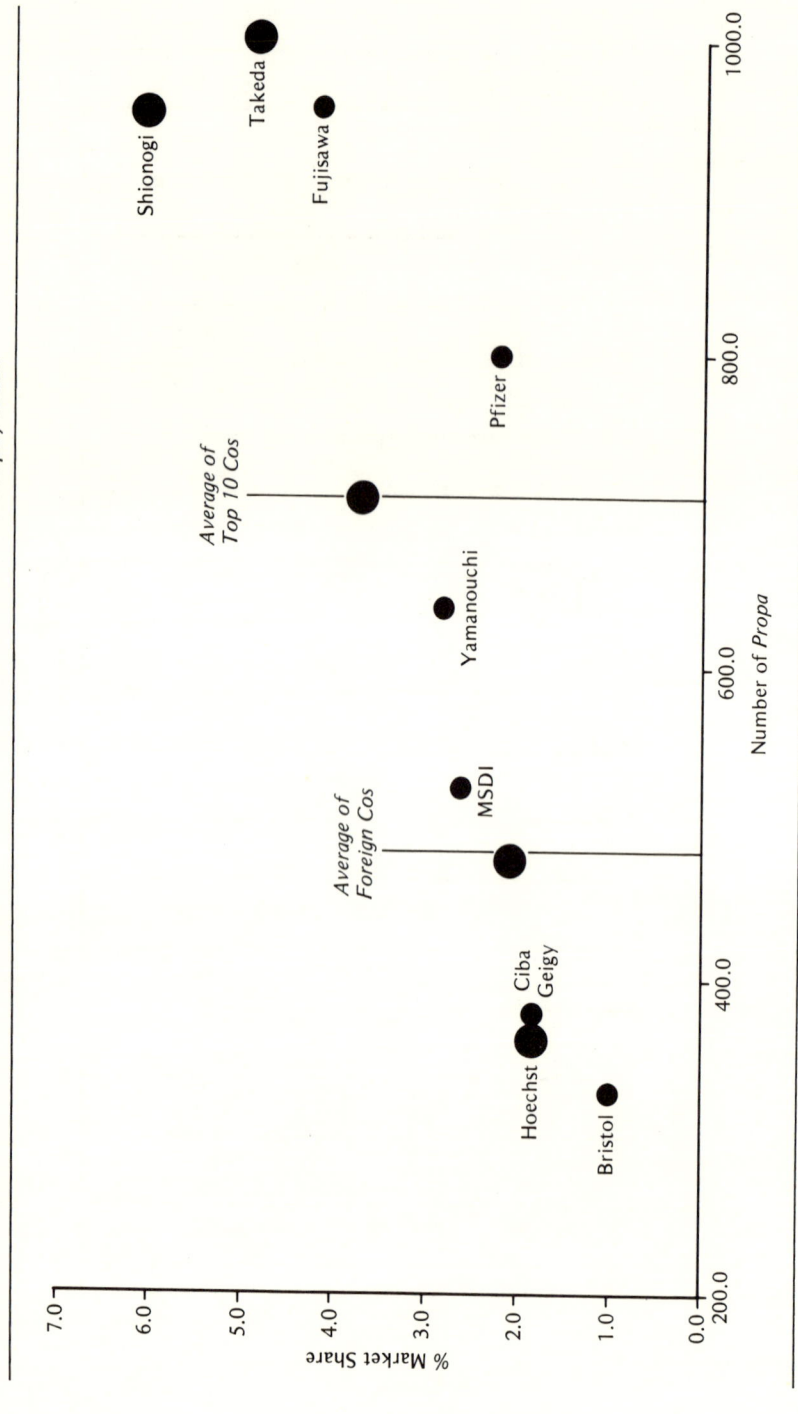

Note: Circle size indicates sales per rep.

be lower than 10 percent because of this dilution. If all their other businesses are taken into account, these companies are often much larger than the pharmaceutical sales figures cited above.

Figure 9-2 shows the relationship between the Japanese pharmaceutical market share vis-à-vis the number of sales representatives or *propa* among a sample of Japanese and Western companies in 1983. These companies were selected on a random basis. From Figure 9-2, there appears to be a direct correlation between the number of sales representatives and their sales efficiency. The size of the circle in the figure indicates the relative dollars worth of pharmaceuticals sold per *propa*. Consequently, the larger the dot or circle, the greater the sales efficiency of the company given. It is apparent that Shionogi, Takeda, and Fujisawa are more efficient than the other companies shown. It appears that the average firm shown, which has approximately 3.5 percent market share, requires a critical mass of about 700 sales representatives to be effective. Merck's relative position does not look favorable but it is due to the fact that we front-loaded our sales force. Many representatives were hired (about 75 to 100 representatives a year) since 1976 to try to build up a strong force to sell the new products that we have exported for introduction into the market in the near future. We are confident that we will not retain this technical appearance of inefficiency for long.

FOREIGN COMPANIES' STRATEGIES IN THE JAPANESE PHARMACEUTICAL MARKETS

Although there are many foreign pharmaceutical companies in Japan, most of which are on a joint venture basis, each has less than 3 percent of the market share. In Table 9-1 we see that there is an increasing trend toward self-sufficiency of foreign pharmaceutical companies in Japan. Six companies are becoming independent in Japan: Beecham, Ciba-Geigy, Glaxo, Pfizer, Roche, and Schering. Merck has a majority equity ownership in two companies.

All foreign companies combined have only about 13 percent of the total Japanese pharmaceutical market. In other words, they have not been a significant factor in the Japanese pharmaceutical market. So the question is: What strategies are appropriate in Japan?

This depends upon the company's corporate culture and specific objectives in Japan. There is a great diversity of thought and opinion

Table 9-1. Major Foreign Corporations in the Japanese Market (*ethical pharmaceuticals*), 1983.

Company	Market Share	Joint Venture Dependency on Japanese Distribution	Independent	Major Equity in Local Company
Abbott	0.3	X		
Astra	< 0.1	X		
American Home Products	< 0.1	X		
Bayer	1.0	X		
Beecham	0.2		X	
Boehringer	0.9	X		
Bristol	1.1	X		
Ciba Geigy	1.8		X	
Essex	0.5	X		
Glaxo	0.3		X	
Hoechst	1.2	X		
ICI	0.5	X		
Johnson & Johnson	< 0.1	X		
Lederle	1.1	X		
Lilly	< 0.1	X		
Merck & Co. Inc.	1.3[a]	X		X
Pfizer	2.2		X	
Rhone Poulenc	< 0.1	X		
Roche	0.3		X	
Rohrer	< 0.1	X		
Roussel Uclaf	0.6	X		
Sandoz	1.2	X		
Schering	0.5		X	
Searle	0.5	X		
SmithKline	0.9	X		
Squibb	0.2	X		
Syntex	0.3	X		
Travenol	0.2	X		
Upjohn	0.8	X		
Warner Lambert	0.1	X		
Wellcome	0.1	X		
Wyeth	< 0.1	X		

a. Prior to August 1983, the market share of Nippon Merck Banyu (NMB) was 1.3 percent. After the acquisitions of Torii and Banyu, the consolidated market shares of the companies was 3.2 percent.

on how to achieve success in Japan, as shown by the different types of commitments made by the various foreign companies.

The Past

After World War II Japan's economy was in a sad state of disrepair. The pharmaceutical industry was particularly hard pressed because the people suffered from poor nutrition, and tuberculosis was rampant. Streptomycin, a Merck product, was introduced around this time and was considered a wonder drug. Since Japan had a good background in fermentation from the brewing of saki and beer, it was natural for them to get into the fermentation of antibiotics. Merck, among others, helped two Japanese pharmaceutical companies get into the manufacture of antibiotics. The pharmaceutical industry in Japan started by providing for the immediate needs of its own country, that is, getting the population healthy. The role of foreign companies at that time was primarily to help the Japanese establish their industry. Subsequently, some joint ventures were formed. Most foreign companies, however, were not too active at that time.

The second phase, from 1965 to 1975, marked an important period because Japanese companies had reached the point where they were quite self-sufficient and could begin to spend money to license new drugs. They were not conducting much research at that time, however. Foreign companies were committed to enter Japan through joint ventures, which were limited to a maximum equity share of 50 percent. Merck had a 49.5 percent share in their joint venture until 1976. In 1970 foreign companies were allowed to set up wholly owned subsidiaries in Japan. From the mid-1970s on, many foreign companies formed joint ventures, but the shares of most ventures remained evenly divided between the Japanese and foreign partners.

Ten years ago there was no foreign pharmaceutical company that operated a wholly owned subsidiary to sell drugs. There were companies, such as Merck Sharp and Dohme (MSD) Japan, which were 100 percent owned companies, but, MSD Japan was not an operating company designed to market and distribute pharmaceuticals. This company was a Merck administration center designed to carry out negotiations on licensing, marketing developments, and the coordination of business activities with Merck corporate headquarters in the United States.

Beginning in 1976 the Japanese companies increased their spending on R&D substantially. As mentioned previously, it used to be less than 5 percent of sales turnover. Now it is 7 to 10 percent of sales turnover, which compares very favorably with R&D expenditures by leading U.S., German, and Swiss pharmaceutical companies.

The Present

At present foreign pharmaceutical companies adopt varied approaches in doing business in Japan. Some have an interest in conventional joint ventures, others in limited joint ventures, and still others in cross-licensing. Cross-licensing is currently popular because the Japanese are unwilling to license a product for a mere royalty. They now prefer to have a new product in exchange for theirs. Therefore, we have these quid pro quo arrangements.

During the past several years MSD licensed several new products from Japan and, in exchange, gave the Japanese companies marketing rights for specific Merck products. For example, Merck licensed a chicken pox vaccine, an oral antibiotic, and an antiulcer drug from major Japanese pharmaceutical companies. These three products are regarded as important additions to our product mix.

In general, foreign pharmaceutical companies in Japan have the following five options: licensing, joint ventures, direct distribution with an independent sales force, codevelopment and comarketing of a specific product, and acquisition of a majority equity position in an established Japanese company. The choice of the appropriate strategy depends on what the foreign company wants to achieve in Japan. Licensing is attractive if the firm has a suitable product and simply wishes to maximize the profitability on that product.

Joint ventures may be of two kinds, conventional or limited, either in terms of time or confined to specific products. Limited joint ventures are becoming more popular because this allows a Japanese company to work with two or three foreign companies and vice versa. I think we will see more "marriages" of the Takeda-Abbott model between Japanese and foreign companies. The Takeda joint venture in the United States appears to be a good one and permits the marketing of Takeda products in the United States, but Takeda is free to enter into business arrangements with other companies. The same applies to Abbott. Abbott does not have worldwide marketing rights for Takeda's products, however. This is true for Merck's own relationships as well. We bought majority equity ownership in Banyu, but we are discussing licensing prospects with other major Japanese companies. As mentioned previously, we have licensed, and will continue to license products from other Japanese companies if the situation is mutually beneficial.

The third strategy, direct distribution with an independent sales force, involves the establishment of an autonomous company. This is essentially what Pfizer has done by buying out its joint venture. This is also what Ciba-Geigy and five other previously mentioned companies will be doing. They will continue to utilize the Japanese wholesaling network even though their sales forces will detail their products directly to physicians. The wholesaler's role in Japan, while complex, does not normally involve detailing. The wholesaler stocks several product lines and fills orders received from doctors. Nevertheless, the wholesaler can be and is very influential. Some wholesalers simply fill orders received, while others promote products to doctors. A key problem for any foreign company is to learn the intricacies of the distribution and sales network and to make the wholesaling organizations a major influential factor for their products. It is often difficult for a foreign company to deal with wholesalers as effectively as a Takeda, a Shionogi, or a Fujisawa. It is not impossible, however. Pfizer, for example, has done very well in this regard.

A fourth strategy for foreign companies in Japan is codeveloping and comarketing a specific product. This is a very attractive option because the risk can be spread, particularly if the company has a minor product with limited sales potential. In other cases, comarketing can result in gaining a larger market share for major products. The cost of development and marketing is shared by both parties. Both partners gain because they are engaged in a product venture that may not have been worthwhile for either company to develop and market on its own. One partner may have better marketing capability; the other may have better developmental knowledge. Presently, Merck is comarketing a few major products in Japan. An example is Clinoril, an arthritis drug, which is comarketed effectively in Japan by Banyu (Merck) and Kyorin to achieve a major market share. Although comarketing is a good strategy for a specific product, it does not appear to be the best way to establish a broader business base in Japan.

A fifth strategy is acquisition of the majority equity share of an established Japanese company. This is what Merck has done. We felt, and continue to feel, that it has all the advantages of a joint venture in terms of having Japanese people who know the government agencies, have established the right contacts and personal relationships, and have a tie into the distribution and wholesaling networks. This is truly a marriage. Mr. Reed Maurer, Merck's vice-president for Japan, has referred to this as "teaming." He prefers the term "teaming" because he wants to differentiate this from a joint venture. It is truly a team effort because it is inside Japan as a Japanese company. If a foreign firm becomes an independent entity in Japan, it is not considered a "Japanese company." However, teaming is not a viable option unless the firm wants to stay in Japan for a long time. It is very difficult to divest from an acquisition or joint venture.

Merck recognizes all the short-term difficulties that may be associated with this approach, such as the problems of integrating and consolidating two established organizations. However, we also recognize that, in the long term, Banyu will evolve as a solid and more powerful Japanese company backed by the strong research capability of Merck. The flow of many new products into this truly Japanese company, which continues to be managed by Merck's leaders, will certainly bring about a very positive result for both Banyu and Merck and Company, Inc.

The Future

The choice of the appropriate strategy depends on the company's short- and long-term objectives and on what the company expects of their Japanese business. Is the purpose to obtain major market share? Merck is interested in obtaining a major share of the Japanese pharmaceutical business. We want to break the 7 percent market share barrier if we can. At present we have a little over 3 percent share of the Japanese pharmaceutical business, if we consolidate the shares of the Merck group consisting of Banyu, Torii, and MSD Japan.

If a company wants to maximize the profitability of a single product, then it certainly would not want to go this route. It should either codevelop, comarket, or license its product.

Other important consideration is long- versus short-term expectations. This is where joint ventures often get into trouble. The partners may have different goals. If the Japanese management has long-term goals and the foreign company has short-term objectives and wants to achieve immediate profitability, one would, of course, expect a conflict.

The independent company approach has advantages because it allows the foreign company to have complete control over marketing, production, and R&D, but the firm still has to depend on the complicated Japanese distribution and wholesaling system. Even though a foreign company can hire its own sales force to detail its drugs to physicians, it still has to rely on effective wholesalers to actually make the sale.

Another consideration for a foreign company is to gain a majority equity position in a joint venture. This is a sound approach if a firm has considerable capital to invest and is really serious about Japan. A firm should not go this route unless it is truly committed for the long term.

Another positive element for foreign companies in Japan is the new technology that is being developed. If a company is in Japan, either as a joint venture or in a majority equity position, it has much more ready access to licensing opportunities. It is virtually impossible to send Americans or other foreigners to Japan on one or more trips and have them talk to twenty companies and come back with several licensing candidates. You must have Japanese speaking and communicating effectively with Japanese over a period of time to be successful.

In short, the strategies available to foreign firms depend on the companies' objectives and their corporate philosophies. The outlook for business relationships in Japan in the future is multifaceted. The future for the pharmaceutical industry will be one where there are many types of interrelationships, and they are not all going to be easily classified. It is going to be a mixed bag. The future will not clearly favor joint ventures or licensing or a majority equity position arrangement. It may be a mixture of two or three arrangements. In the case of Merck, we have three or four relationships going on simultaneously. The choice of the appropriate strategy depends upon the product and what we expect to achieve in return.

The major multinationals will certainly become more actively involved in Japan since it is such a huge market. Given the fact that Japan is a wealthy, health-conscious nation and represents such a large share of the world pharmaceutical market, it will continue to attract foreign companies.

The foreign pharmaceutical companies and their Japanese counterparts will become more interactive on a worldwide basis. Japan will play a more dominant role in the future and we will see more of the Japanese companies in the United States and Europe. At present foreign companies are selling many Japanese products under license. In the future, however, we will see a direct Japanese presence in the United States. This is an exciting challenge for both foreign and Japanese companies. We do not anticipate that the pharmaceutical industry will parallel the automotive industry, as it is not a labor- and capital-intensive industry. The pharmaceutical business is a high technology industry, and there is no reason why the Japanese should have any advantage over the major U.S. and European companies.

We believe that our research at Merck continues to be our future, as it has been for over fifty years. We are also committed to Japan and want to see success there. While the future in the pharmaceutical industry will continue to depend upon research, research, and more research, effective multinational sales and marketing will be a requisite to maximizing the profitability of successful companies.

10 MANAGEMENT PRACTICES AND BUSINESS STRATEGY IN MANUFACTURING FIRMS

Vladimir Pucik

In the past five years the success of many Japanese manufacturers in penetrating markets around the world, in particular the United States, resulted in an explosion of interest in Japanese management practices. In many cases, Westerners were exhorted to adopt Japanese methods as quickly as possible, but there were also some who dismissed and still dismiss Japan's record as some kind of conspiracy to be fought against with all available means. This discussion does not attempt to cast any moral judgments on the merits or limitations of Japanese management practices. Rather, it attempts to illustrate how internal management practices influence the competitive strategies of Japanese manufacturing firms. The chapter analyzes the principal characteristics of Japanese competitive behavior and discusses their implications for U.S. firms.

The notion that structure follows strategy (Chandler 1966) still dominates the literature on business strategy, though some doubts are being raised in this regard. In the Japanese case, however, the strategies of Japanese manufacturing firms are clearly driven by structural conditions derived from their basic managerial paradigm: focus on human resources as the key corporate asset. This paradigm translates into specific management practices and techniques, such as the development of an internal labor market, intensive socialization, and long-term appraisal (Pucik and Hatvany 1983), all supporting a pattern of strategic behavior that challenges typical American expectations about competitive behavior in the marketplace.

The focus on human resources implies that the survival of the firm is the ultimate strategic objective. The environment is viewed as essentially hostile and competition all-pervasive. Market share dominance, pursued through aggressive pricing and shifting market segmentation, is indispensable to the long-term survival of the firm. Internal diversification is the sole avenue to growth. Rapid introduction of new products and new technology are essential to remaining in the race.

COMPETITION AS A WAY OF LIFE

Contrary to the popular image of "Japan, Inc.," where the government and private industry support each other and where oligopolistic collusion of dominant firms is tolerated, if not encouraged, competition among Japanese firms is very keen. Although large firms seldom go out of business because of their strong ties to the financial community, the bankruptcy rate in Japan is still twice as high as that in the United States. Most formal and informal cartel arrangements are established to prevent firms from pursuing strategies of mutual destruction which could bring havoc on the entire economy.

In this environment it is fair to say that the principal purpose of a Japanese firm is to survive as a social group—a task possible only through "besting" its present and potential rivals, both in Japan and overseas. The world outside the firm is perceived in terms of friends and foes and of markets to be captured or defended. As such, there is no contradiction between survival and profit-oriented strategies. Profits are essential for survival in order to attract and reward investors and to provide resources for continuous growth.

The need to survive is an economic imperative driven by the characteristics of the Japanese labor market. A loss of jobs resulting from a business failure is very costly to most employees, particularly those at the higher levels. In general, the higher the status, the bigger the potential loss. Managers have more at stake than rank-and-file employees because alternative job opportunities at similar wages are generally not available. This is because most large employers who offer the highest salaries prefer to hire only new college graduates.

Mid-career job openings are limited and are generally concentrated in low-paying small and medium-sized enterprises and in subsidiaries of foreign firms.

This survival orientation is constantly reinforced through an intensive socialization of all employees. The socialization process begins when they enter the firm and continues throughout their working lives. As a result, the organization develops a distinct identity based on a clearly articulated company philosophy and a strong corporate culture which emphasizes all-pervasive competition as a way of life.

Japanese employees, and managers in particular, are brought up in an atmosphere of competitive rivalry that eventually permeates every action and decision they make. The activities of the firm are continuously scrutinized with respect to its impact on major competitors. Intensive defensive and offensive scouting is built into all external operations and gathered intelligence, accompanied by summaries highlighting its consequences for future market battles, is distributed widely throughout the organization.

Often, the foreign market strategies of Japanese firms are products of the competitive circumstances at home. For example, the heavy emphasis on exporting by relative newcomers in their respective fields, such as Sony in the case of consumer electronics and Honda in the automotive industry, was largely due to the difficulties encountered in competing with established domestic producers.

Business strategy is often driven by a desire to prevent rivals from gaining market position, regardless of the broader consequences of such competitive tactics. A situation where no one makes any money is preferable to losing market share to competitors. As a result, overcapacity is endemic in a number of Japanese industries, leading to a severe price war and export expansion. The motorcycle, video recorder, and memory chips industries are recent examples of this type of situation.

LONG-TERM PERSPECTIVE

The concern with survival of the firm in a very competitive environment determines the time frame of long-term corporate strategies. In this respect, the term "long-term" does not stand for any explicit time period as determined by a strategic planning framework. Rather, it reflects an implicit assumption that the function of business strategy is to enhance the firm's chances for survival. This is the ultimate long-term measure of success, one that is understandable to all.

It is not, as often thought, superior long-term planning per se that enables the Japanese to execute successful investment strategies. In fact, the planning methodology used by a typical Japanese firm is generally not very sophisticated by Western standards. Most Japanese firms do not use planning tools, such as discounted cash flow analysis. Financial criteria, other than desired payback period, are seldom used for decisionmaking. Expected cash flow and return on investment are used for purposes of financial planning, but they are considered of secondary importance in strategy selection (Nonaka and Okumura 1984).

In Japan the strategic objective is expressed in terms of market position or introduction of new technology (Kono 1984). The investment selection process is guided primarily by a qualitative evaluation of potential gains in market position compared with the costs of a weakened position in case of no investment. This allows for considerable flexibility in the implementation stage. For example, in the early 1960s Honda's initial strategy for the U.S. motorcycle market was the introduction of large models. Because of quality problems and marketing mistakes, the initial sales campaign was unsuccessful. Within months the strategy was shifted to emphasize small motorcycles. However, the overall mission, which was to obtain a 10 percent share of the U.S. market, was not changed.

The commitment to long-term strategic objectives is encouraged by an absence of short-term incentives that may distract managers from the pursuit of long-term goals. Strategy implementation is not tied to short-term financial criteria, even though financial discipline is tight. Long-term compensation plans for executives and managers are not used. Bonuses computed as a multiple of base salary are distributed among all employees as a form of quasi profit sharing. Although the total amount available for bonus payout is linked to current corporate performance, the competitive conditions and long-term trends in the marketplace are also considered. Since most employees are expected to remain in the organization for most of their working lives, one cannot escape the consequences of one's decisions. This tends to minimize the danger that an employee will take advantage of current circumstances at the expense of future goals.

In addition, the reliance on the future well-being of the company to provide for individual welfare, coupled with the future-oriented appraisal system, makes it easier to incorporate long-term strategic objectives into the management of everyday operations with a minimum of formality and complexity. There is no need for sophisticated reporting systems which attempt to use complex formulas to direct executives and managers in the proper direction. In this respect, "perseverance" and "commitment" are equal to "harmony" and "team spirit" in the arsenal of desired and rewarded corporate values.

EMPHASIS ON MARKET SHARE

It has often been said that the aggressive market behavior of Japanese firms is enforced by their high fixed costs of production due to a policy of stable employment and a heavy dependence on debt financing. Wages of employees and interest on loans have to be paid irrespective of the sales volume. It follows, then, that in times of business retrenchments, it may be more attractive to slash prices and keep output high than to follow the strategy typical of Western firms, that being to protect profit margins by trimming output and, consequently, employment.

It was pointed out recently that the high debt-equity ratio in Japan relative to other industrialized countries is a reflection of the differences in accounting practices and definitions. It was further noted that if market values of debt and equities are used for calculations, the difference between Japan and other industrialized countries is perhaps much smaller than generally thought (Kuroda and Oritani 1980). In a similar vein, there is evidence that although employment in Japan is relatively stable during recessions, the actual labor costs exhibit greater flexibility than those in the United States (Gordon 1981). In a typical Japanese firm, when demand declines, wages and hours worked are adjusted accordingly, before any layoffs are considered. Besides the labor market and financial structure of a firm, the aggressive market behavior characteristic of most Japanese manufacturing firms can be attributed to several other factors, such as the rivalry among industrial groups and competitive strategies that emphasize market share over short-term profits.

The emphasis on market share fits in well with the Japanese management system, as it supports the emphasis on survival as the key strategic objective. Market share, protected by economies of scale in production and distribution, is seen as more defensible than high margins in limited markets that may be vulnerable to a price attack by a determined competitor. Market share also provides an objective measure of competitive standing—independent of current investment and R&D strategies or changes in depreciation and tax rules—that is clear and understandable to anyone in the organization. At the same time, it has been shown that market share over the long run is a good predictor of corporate performance as expressed in more traditional financial terms (Buzzell, Gale, and Sultan 1975).

Market share strategies are supported by careful market segmentation. However, the purpose of segmentation is not to identify niches where returns higher than the industry average can be achieved. Rather, the objective is to identify a logical sequence of market penetration that leads from one market segment to the product markets as a whole. As many U.S. manufacturers have already painfully learned, the Japanese penetration of high-volume, low value-added segments is only the beginning of a long march to take over other market segments later. The consumer electronics and automobile industries provide the most obvious examples. Furthermore, the market segmentation strategy is not limited to low-end entry. Several Japanese camera manufacturers, for instance, decided to challenge Kodak's dominance by attacking the high end of the camera market first and then push into Kodak's territory by lowering prices through cost reduction based on technological innovation.

Aggressive market penetration is possible because Japanese managers are free to pursue short-term market share gains through incremental or variable cost pricing. Sale prices are dictated by what a new customer is willing to pay. As long as such a price covers incremental costs of the new order, the new business is accepted. The assumption is that continued cost reduction programs, on the one hand, and product improvement efforts, on the other hand, will gradually result in profits on a full cost basis. However, this is not a strategy based on a simple experience curve effect. Volume-related reduction of costs is expected, and the objective is to push the slope of the experience curve down to lower the cost faster than competitors with a similar market share.

A strategy driven by market share considerations also calls for a new look at the product life cycle. Product maturity is interpreted not only in terms of market growth but also with respect to the potential of additional market penetration. In the Japanese view even a mature product market is attractive if market share expansion can be achieved at the expense of current competitors, by introducing products with more advanced features or by investing in low-cost production technology. Bridgestone's entry into the U.S. tire market through investment in local manufacturing at a time when most U.S. producers are reducing capacity is a good example of the latter strategy. Two years after Bridgestone acquired an obsolete manufacturing plant from its U.S. owner and rebuilt it, plant production is at an all-time high and still growing.

From another perspective, Japanese firms are reluctant to divest from existing low growth/low market share situations with the same speed as their U.S. competitors for several reasons. First, such markets are potentially useful to check expansion of a powerful competitor or to launch products not yet invented. Second, the avoidance of disinvestment is also motivated by its negative implications for employment stability. Third, as traditional financial ratios are secondary in importance as measures of performance, divestments for the sake of improving the balance sheet generally do not occur. As a result, Japan lacks the spectacular low tech/high tech transformation undertaken by Gould or IC Industries in the United States, but it also avoids the failure of diversification experienced by Exxon, Mobil, AM International, and numerous other firms exhibiting mergermania.

GROWTH THROUGH INTERNAL DIVERSIFICATION

As noted previously, the organization culture in Japanese firms places a premium on maintaining the corporation as a group of individuals tied together by lasting bonds. For that reason, divestitures, mergers, and acquisitions—especially those involving firms from unrelated industries—are unusual in Japan; furthermore, hostile takeovers are next to impossible (Clark 1979). The strong barriers to mergers and acquisitions are perhaps detrimental to the efficient allocation of resources in the economy. However, once it is clearly established that the only way to grow is from internal competitive strength, the strategic implications are clear: There is no short cut, no other way than concentrating on making a product that meets the needs of the customers and is cheaper and of higher quality than that of competitors. A further advantage of this aversion to acquisitions is that top management can be closely involved with operations, as they and their staff do not have to spend time planning takeover strategies or putting together defenses against them. Given the constraints these takeover planning sessions place on executive time, the acquisition route to growth, which is popular in the United States, may entail substantial opportunity costs, with which their Japanese counterparts do not have to contend.

Under such conditions it is natural that engineering and manufacturing become major strategic concerns in the organization, resulting in an emphasis on continuous product and process innovation and on upgrading quality and lowering costs. There is also a direct correlation between operations-oriented competitive strategies and human resource management practices. In contrast to many U.S. firms, the operations area is viewed as a key to corporate survival and is thus staffed by high-quality managers with good chances of advancing eventually to top executive positions. Among 314 new corporate chief executive officers (CEOs) appointed in 1984, more than 29 percent advanced through manufacturing or engineering and 30 percent through marketing (*Japan Economic Journal* 1985).

In addition, the focus on internal growth permits the organization to pursue strategic changes incrementally so that they can more easily be absorbed by the organization. The "logical incrementalism" advocated by Quinn (1980) is a concept familiar in practice to managers in many Japanese firms. Moreover, internal growth allows the organization to satisfy the career aspirations of many employees by creating vacancies in new areas of business that can be staffed from within. In Japanese industry growth implies the establishment of affiliates and subsidiaries, not the building up of a centralized empire.

Many Japanese manufacturing firms today operate as quasi conglomerates. The parent company maintains direct control over key business groups and divisions and has equity interest in a family of vertically and horizontally integrated subsidiaries and affiliates created through spin-offs from the parent and some of the key subsidiaries. Several of the large affiliates are usually independently listed on the stock exchange. In the case of large firms such as Hitachi or Matsushita, the number of affiliates can reach several hundred, arrayed in several layers of intrafamily hierarchy.

The degree of control within the corporate family is flexible, depending on an affiliate's performance. The faster the growth, the larger the degree of autonomy given to the spin-off firm. It is not uncommon for some spin-offs to outgrow their parents and become the new center of the corporate family, as in the case of Toyota and Fujitsu. The management of the affiliates has, therefore, a great incentive to push aggressively for new areas of business while being protected from at least some of the risk by their intrafamily ties. However, in case of failure, the parent firm will not hesitate to intervene even after years of laissez faire policy. The change in Yamaha Motors' top management under the guidance of Nippon Gakki is the most recent example.

An additional point concerning corporate families in Japan has important implications for market competitiveness. In the case of integrated affiliates, the cost of control is kept at a minimum by avoiding coordination through parent company staff and relying instead on marked enforced discipline and direct coordination among line managers involved in the intrafamily transaction. The cost savings from the elimination of a large number of divisions, groups, sectors, and head office staff can be substantial. In a comparison of U.S. and Japanese automotive firms, such savings were found to reach nearly $200 per car (Pucik 1984).

AGGRESSIVE INNOVATION

As noted elsewhere, the nature of the appraisal system in Japanese firms and the rapid reception and dissemination of new ideas in Japanese firms should encourage innovation (Pucik and Hatvany 1983). When long-term behavior rather than short-term "bottom line" performance is the focus of evaluation, means as well as ends may be assessed. Aversion to risk is minimized and creativity is facilitated both by the assumption of stable employment and by tolerance of honest mistakes in the evaluation process. This combination of security and incentive for challenging assignments creates what Pelz (1967) characterized as a "creative" challenge, an environment suitable for the nurturing of innovations and rapid sharing of new ideas. This notion is contrary to the stereotypic image of the Japanese as poor innovators constrained in their exploration of new frontiers by a group desirous of maintaining consensus and harmony. In this respect, the evidence is clear: The Japanese do innovate as fast as, if not quicker than, most businesses in other countries (Moritani 1981).

One reason for the discrepancy between the stereotype and the reality is the misunderstanding of innovation processes in the organization. It is not only the bright idea that counts, but the process of introducing the product, based on the new idea, to the market. In the competitive game the origin of the idea is often secondary. After all, computers, jet engines, and scanners were not invented in the United States, although U.S. firms enjoy a commanding lead in these product markets. The Japanese have an advantage in the implementation process because they have worldwide monitoring systems, on the outside, and a high level of interface, coordination, and teamwork, on the inside, involving everyone concerned with development, design, and manufacturing. These combined efforts result in the manufacture of carefully built products.

A second reason for the erroneous stereotyping of the Japanese as poor innovators stems from the widely held belief that there is a shortage of venture capital. Because external capital is not available, it is very difficult for Japanese R&D personnel to leave their employers and strike out on their own—a pattern common in the United States. However, a closer look reveals that this limitation may actually work to Japan's advantage.

With their research teams kept from the temptation of windfall profits as independent entrepreneurs, Japanese companies are well poised to capitalize quickly on newly acquired knowledge. Rather than working in the secrecy of the family garage, the Japanese engineer is working on new inventions in the corporate laboratory and has regular communication with those responsible for its future commercial adaptation. Then, once an innovative idea proves to be promising, the organization can move quickly to the adoption phase, as everyone concerned is already familiar with the new product's characteristics. In other words, although the Japanese may lag behind in the "discovery" stage, they more than catch up during the phase of product commercialization.

Close cooperation and communication between the research engineers, on the one side, and production and marketing personnel, on the other, is built into the Japanese management system. This greatly facilitates the communication of new innovations and ensures the integration of research and development with other critical corporate functions. A steady feedback of market information to the research personnel enhances the likelihood that research and development will result in products that meet market needs.

The participation of production engineers in the development process increases the likelihood that the newly designed product can be built efficiently with available production technologies or new technologies that will be available shortly. Thus, rather than remaining an exclusive domain of R&D professionals, the innovation process is diffused widely throughout the organization, enlarging the strategic alternatives available to the firm.

IMPLICATIONS FOR U.S. FIRMS

Many U.S. firms entering the Japanese market are unaware of its competitive intensity. Their business plans are developed in accordance with their U.S. or European experiences, allocating resources insufficient to withstand the counterattack from their Japanese competitors. U.S. firms also underestimate the need for collecting competitive intelligence and, as a result, often end up in alliances with Japanese partners who have no real desire or capacity to promote the strategic interest of their foreign partner, as in the case of the partnership between Apple Computer and the giant synthetic fiber manufacturer, Toray, or in the home appliance business between Whirlpool and Sony. Not surprisingly, both partnerships totally failed to help the U.S. firms penetrate the market in Japan.

The lack of knowledge about the patterns of competition in Japan leads many foreign firms to believe that they are up against "Japan Inc." Such a simplistic view prevents them from recognizing conflicting interests among their Japanese counterparts and building successful alliances for the penetration of markets in Japan. IBM's success in Japan is largely due to a strategic alliance with the Mitsubishi group companies which lack a computer manufacturer of their own. The support of IBM enables the Mitsubishi group firms to strengthen their competitive position against firms from industrial groups such as Sumitomo, DKB, or Fuyo, which have strong ties to NEC, Fujitsu, and Hitachi.

The long-term strategic perspective of Japanese firms is apparent in the different ways that Japanese and Western firms view joint ventures and other kinds of technological and marketing tie-ups. The Japanese perceive such relationships as temporary arrangements to rectify some of their competitive weakness and which should, in the long run, lead to their dominance in the partnership. Foreign firms are generally content with the short-term gains from such endeavors and don't consider the long-term competitive consequences.

This perceptual difference does not mean that a long-term mutually advantageous relationship with Japanese partners is impossible. It can be done, but only as long as a long-term competitive parity is maintained. Contractual protection, such as limitation of exports, will not hold under Japanese antitrust law, as many U.S. firms found out to their dismay (Zimmerman 1985). In several cases, after the technology transfer was completed, the U.S. firms were forced to amend the export-restricting agreements with their Japanese partners under the threat of a unilateral contract cancellation by the Japanese government. A more promising joint venture strategy is to choose a Japanese partner with complementary, rather than competing, long-term strategic interests.

For most Japanese firms, market share is ultimately a worldwide concept. To retreat from a market territory or a product segment under challenge from a Japanese competitor will therefore do nothing more than buy time before the remaining markets also fall under siege. To "niche" away from the Japanese is a fantasy proven fatal to a great many U.S. firms. As soon as the Japanese develop a comparable product, and given their propensity for aggressive pricing, a typical U.S. firm that limits its strategy to defense of the domestic market is very vulnerable (Hamel and Prahalad 1985). The decline of U.S. home electronics is a classic though still unheeded example. First, the U.S. manufacturers abandoned the audio market to Japan, followed by a retreat from black-and-white televisions. Defeat in color televisions came next. Finally, the boom in video cassette recorders and in compact disk technology left the remaining U.S. manufacturers on the sidelines. Most of them now survive only on allocations of products from their Japanese competitors to be marketed under the U.S. brand names.

An equally self-defeating strategy can be an attempt to piggyback the success of Japanese manufacturers and use them as original equipment manufacturer (OEM) suppliers for domestically well-established brands. Sooner or later they will go it alone, leaving only crumbs for their former partner. This is the lesson GE learned in their audio business. Faced with price competition, GE began to purchase low-cost parts from its competitors. Eventually, most of the critical components were sourced from Japan. However, when a new generation of products appeared, Japanese vendors limited the supply of the upgraded components to GE, forcing it to choose between losing market share or purchasing finished products on an OEM basis. The next stage, GE's retreat from the audio business, is now just a question of time. Again, the only way to secure a fruitful long-term cooperation is to maintain competitive parity with the Japanese partner.

The frequent reliance of U.S. firms on niche-based competitive strategies to defend themselves against the Japanese often rests on a naïve assumption that the U.S. firm will be able to maintain a permanent technological leadership. However, given the rapidity of technological change, such an assumption is presumptuous in the long run. Without an appropriate competitive leverage in manufacturing and distribution, one or two snags in the development effort will bury the firm. The confident statements of the past that the Japanese would never be able to catch up in advanced microchip designs present a dramatic contrast to current difficulties encountered in the U.S. semiconductor industry.

CONCLUSION

The reality of market competition is simple. The issue is not whether Japanese management practices are transferable to the United States. Many of them are, as demonstrated by the success of Japanese-owned U.S. subsidiaries. However, in order to be competitive in world markets with Japanese firms, U.S. companies have to more than rejuvenate their management culture along some version of the Japanese model or its U.S. "Z" or "excellence" equivalents. U.S. firms have to develop a better understanding of Japanese competitive strategies and respond to them in a proactive manner. In particular, the U.S. firms have to switch from niche-based product strategies to a new competitive posture based on integrated and leveraged portfolio of products and technologies. The internal control system has to allow flexible and aggressive pricing and encourage penetration of foreign markets. Ultimately, an active presence in the Japanese market is the best long-term defense.

Observing Japanese worldwide strategies, it is not difficult to notice that they are carefully designed to take maximum advantage of Japanese strengths, such as human resources and manufacturing management. They are also designed to capitalize on the shortcomings of their foreign competitors. There is no great magic to this approach. What is required to match the Japanese challenge is to take a hard, common sense look on how we plan and implement our competitive game plan. The first step is to acknowledge the capabilities of our competitors. What has to follow is the elimination of outdated practices that hinder our capacity to compete. The enemy is not in Tokyo; it is in us. In the final analysis, it is important to note that relief will not come from politicians in Washington. We are the ones that have to change.

REFERENCES

Buzzell, Robert D.; Bradley T. Gale; and Ralph G.M. Sultan. 1975. "Market Share: A Key to Profitability." *Harvard Business Review* 53, no. 1: 97–106.

Chandler, Alfred D., Jr. 1966. *Strategy and Structure.* New York: Doubleday.

Clark, Rodney C. 1979. *The Japanese Company.* New Haven: Yale University Press.

Gordon, Robert J. 1981. Working Paper No. 809. "Why U.S. Wage and Employment Behavior Differs from That in Britain and Japan?" Cambridge, Mass.: National Bureau of Economic Research.

Hamel, Gary, and C.K. Prahalad. 1985. "Do You Really Have a Global Strategy?" *Harvard Business Review* 85, no. 4: 139–48.

Japan Economic Journal. 1985. "New Presidents 58 Years Old on Average." June 25: 29.

Kono, Toyohiro. 1984. *Structure and Strategy of Japanese Enterprises.* Armonk, N.Y.: M.E. Sharpe.

Kuroda, Iwao, and Yoshiharu Oritani. 1980. "A Re-Examination of the Unique Features of Japan's Corporate Financial Structure." *Japanese Economic Studies* 8, no. 4: 82–117.

Moritani, Masanori. 1981. *Japanese Technology: Getting the Best for the Least.* Tokyo: Simul Press.

Nonaka, Ikujiro, and Akihiro Okumura. 1984. "A Comparison of Management in American, Japanese and European Firms." *Management Japan* 17, nos. 1 and 2: pp. 23–40 and 20–27.

Pelz, Donald C. 1967. "Creative Tensions in the Research and Development Climate." *Science* 194: 160-65.
Pucik, Vladimir. 1984. "White Collar Human Resource Management: A Comparison of the U.S. and Japanese Automobile Industries." *Columbia Journal of World Business* 19, no. 3: 87-94.
Pucik, Vladimir, and Nina Hatvany. 1983. "Management Practices in Japan and Their Impact on Business Strategy." In *Advances in Strategic Management*, edited by Robert B. Lamb, pp. 103-31. Greenwich, Conn.: JAI Press.
Quinn, James B. 1980. *Strategies for Change: Logical Incrementalism.* Homewood, Ill.: Irwin.
Rohlen, Thomas P. 1974. *For Harmony and Strength: Japanese White-Collar Organization in Anthropological Perspective.* Berkeley: University of California Press.
Zimmerman, Mark. 1985. *How To Do Business with the Japanese: A Strategy for Success.* New York: Random House.

IV STRATEGIC MANAGEMENT IN THE FINANCIAL SECTOR

11 A COMPARATIVE ANALYSIS OF CORPORATE CAPITAL STRUCTURE IN THE UNITED STATES AND JAPAN

William H. Davidson

This chapter analyzes comparative financial ratios for Japanese and U.S. manufacturing corporations. Aggregate financial ratios for the entire U.S. and Japanese manufacturing sectors are included in this study. Because of the distinct financial profile of primary or "first-tier" Japanese companies, however, this study focuses on a sample of 266 major U.S. and Japanese corporations (see Appendix 11A for a listing of the companies). These companies represent the largest firms from both countries in thirty-nine broadly defined industries. All the companies in this sample have sales exceeding $500 million. Although the sample is small and includes only the very largest industrial firms in the two countries, it can provide insights into differences between U.S. and Japanese companies' financial structure, philosophy, and performance. Observations from this analysis can also be linked to differences in the structure and function of capital markets in the two countries and the overall performance of these two economic systems.

SOURCES OF INDUSTRIAL FUNDS

Japanese firms utilize the full range of funding options to meet their financial requirements. Equity sales, bond issues, bank borrowings, and operating cash flow all play a role as sources of funds. However, as Table 11-1 shows, internally generated funds account for a much smaller share of total funds sources for the sample of 95 Japanese firms (51.7 percent) than the sample of 171 U.S. firms (65.3 percent). In contrast to the U.S. corporations, depreciation accounts for virtually all internal funds sources for this sample of Japanese companies. Retained earnings totaled only 6 percent of internal funds sources in 1981, the remainder being derived from depreciation. This high depreciation figure stems from more liberal depreciation rules and higher fixed asset-intensity in Japan. The small retained earnings portion of internal sources relative to U.S. firms also reflects a dramatic difference in profitability. This difference in profitability holds important implications in assessing the competitive positions of U.S. and Japanese industry.

Japanese firms operate at significantly lower rates of return than their U.S. counterparts. This distinction is apparent in aggregate data and for the specific sample analyzed here. For the sample of 266 firms, the average return on sales, assets, and equity are significantly lower for Japanese firms than their U.S. counterparts (see Table 11-2). Returns on assets for U.S. firms (7.4 percent) are three times higher than for the Japanese companies (2.8 percent); returns on equity for Japanese firms (12.1 percent), however, approach those for U.S. firms (15.4 percent). This distinction is due primarily to the higher level of debt utilization in Japan. The majority of debt on Japanese balance sheets stems from bank borrowings.

Bank borrowings accounted for a predominant share (86.4 percent) of total external funding in 1981. The large majority of these borrowings (72.8 percent of total external funds) came from private financial institutions. Government financial institutions played only a limited role, supplying just 10.8 percent of total borrowing. The issue of new equity and bonds have never been prevalent ways of raising funds in Japan; the two combined contributed only 13.6 percent of total sources of funds in 1981 (see Table 11-1). However, these secondary sources play a more important role than it appears. Funds from equity, bonds, and government financial institutions total about half of all investments in property, plant, and equipment. There is a strong relationship between these sources of funds and fixed asset investments. Government loans have accounted for 15 to 20 percent of such funds; equity 10 to 15 percent; and bonds from 15 to 20 percent, on average, over the past ten years (Bank of Japan figures, various years). The longer the time horizon of investments,

Table 11-1. Source of Funds for U.S. and Japanese Manufacturing Corporations.

	1965-1975 Average	1975-1978 Average	1979	1980	1981
All Japanese Manufacturing Companies					
External					
Equity	3.3%	3.5%	3.6%	3.3%	6.3%
Borrowings	32.0	20.4	10.7	13.3	14.2
Bonds	6.5	7.3	4.0	3.0	5.9
Internal					
Depreciation	46.4%	55.5	67.4	61.3	59.2
Retained earnings	8.5	8.4	12.6	17.2	13.4

	1970	1975	1979	1981
95 Japanese Corporations				
External sources				
Equity	4.0 %	3.7 %	3.5 %	4.4 %
Bonds	1.4	3.7	2.3	2.2
Borrowings	44.7	47.7	35.3	41.7
Subtotal	49.7	55.1	41.1	48.3
Internal sources				
Depreciation	20.2	41.7	49.2	48.9
Retained earnings	30.0	3.3	9.6	2.9
Subtotal	50.2	44.9	58.9	51.7
Index (1970 = 100)	100	140	155	192
171 U.S. Corporations				
External sources	39.6	23.7	45.5	34.4
Internal sources	60.4	76.3	54.5	65.6
Index (1970 = 100)	100	154.9	343.3	349.2

Sources: Research and Statistics Department, Bank of Japan, "Features of Recent Corporate Financing," Special Paper No. 100, 1982, p. 17; Ministry of International Trade and Industry, *Sekai Kigyo No Keiei Bunseki*, various years.

Table 11-2. Comparative Financial Ratios for U.S. and Japanese Firms in Seven Manufacturing Industries, 1981.

		Overall	Ordinary Steel	Office and Business Machines	Electronic Machinery	Household Electronic Apparatus	Computer Electronics	Automobile	Ship-building
Profit/sales (%)	A	2.5	3.4	4.2	2.8	3.7	3.2	3.5	-0.2
	B	5.1	3.1	10.8	5.9	5.5	11.9	2.4	1.6
Current ratio (%)	A	112.1	9.50	149.1	119.9	116.3	121.9	127.4	124.3
	B	158.7	161.9	207.7	134.1	241.5	181.5	167.8	163.7
Debt/total assets (%)	A	24.1	40.8	12.6	12.4	9.5	24.0	8.6	25.9
	B	22.4	29.0	14.9	14.5	22.9	13.6	13.5	36.1
Debt/net worth (%)	A	104.4	276.8	32.0	60.8	20.8	89.0	17.2	252.4
	B	46.8	58.4	24.8	34.7	45.3	22.8	26.8	128.4
Debt/capitalization (%)	A	51.1	73.5	24.2	37.8	17.2	47.1	14.7	71.6
	B	31.9	36.9	19.9	25.7	31.2	18.6	21.1	56.1
Net worth/assets (%)	A	23.1	14.7	39.4	20.4	45.8	27.0	49.9	10.3
	B	47.9	48.7	60.2	41.8	50.5	59.7	50.5	28.2
Asset turnover (times)	A	1.10	0.71	1.33	1.02	1.34	1.00	1.76	0.56
	B	1.45	1.32	1.05	1.27	1.41	0.95	1.96	2.04
Fixed asset turnover (times)	A	2.71	1.23	4.65	3.97	2.80	2.49	3.74	2.52
	B	2.83	2.06	2.37	3.40	4.21	2.04	4.06	1.28
Inventory turnover (times)	A	6.33	4.35	7.85	3.91	11.84	4.27	30.85	2.06
	B	7.55	8.77	5.48	7.00	4.50	8.20	7.69	8.94

Working capital/sales (%)	A	5.8	—	17.8	12.7	5.4	10.8	6.5	28.9
	B	12.0	10.0	25.5	11.7	26.8	22.9	7.3	11.2
ROA (%)	A	2.8	2.4	5.7	2.9	4.9	3.2	6.1	0.7
	B	7.4	4.1	11.3	2.0	7.8	11.2	4.8	3.3
ROE (%)	A	12.1	16.1	14.4	14.1	10.7	11.8	12.3	6.9
	B	15.4	8.2	18.9	18.1	15.3	18.8	9.5	11.8
A/R collection period (days)	A	81.7	68.3	82.3	93.7	68.5	76.8	59.7	184.2
	B	46.4	40.8	71.4	61.7	63.6	78.7	24.7	33.4
Interest coverage (times)	A	2.20	1.82	8.62	3.45	4.46	2.84	8.81	0.12
	B	—	3.78	14.56	8.11	7.21	24.20	5.81	4.09
/Profit (%)	A	29.8	30.9	21.5	31.2	21.5	35.4	19.4	88.6
	B	59.9	74.5	33.5	51.8	37.0	47.1	68.4	186.2

Note: A–Japan
B–United States
Source: Ministry of International Trade and Industry, *Sekai Kigyo No Keiei Bunseki*, 1982.

the more importance bonds, equity, and government financial institutions play in financing them. This trend appears even more significant if we limit our analysis to the largest private firms. For example, bond issues accounted for 6 percent of all external funds for Japanese industry as a whole between 1965 and 1980, but bond issues accounted for 19.1 percent of external funds for the sample of "principal enterprises" surveyed over the years by the Bank of Japan in its annual "Short-Term Economic Survey of Principal Enterprises." The single largest source of funds, however, is private financial institutions, chief among which are the thirteen city banks. These institutions are the key suppliers of short-term funds.

FINANCIAL INSTITUTIONS

The city banks, while assuming responsibility to provide private industries with financial resources, have themselves been chronically worried about fund shortages. Government regulations limit their ability to expand their source of funds by opening new branches or by developing more attractive financial packages for potential depositors. In recent years the city banks have been required to subscribe to a large share of government bond issues (30 percent of total flotation), which has strained the banks' financial position. The implicit obligation of government bond subscriptions has squeezed the city banks' liquidity. As a result, the city banks have increasingly relied on open markets to meet their needs, particularly short-term needs. The Bank of Japan plays a key role here. Bank of Japan loans are made to all banks, including trust banks and long-term credit banks. savings associations, short-term credit dealers, securities companies, and so forth. The predominant majority of the loans, usually 75 percent of the total amount, however, goes to city banks. With this "overloaning" situation the Bank of Japan solidifies its position to guide the city banks.

The city banks rely also on regional banks and agricultural cooperatives to meet their fund requirements. These two types of institutions have superb retail networks to solicit deposits but are in a relatively weak position to attract large borrowers. The city banks, to fulfill very short-term requirements, are also active in the call loan market (lendings and borrowings of funds between financial institutions for very short periods), the bill discount market, and *gensaki* market (bond trading with repurchase agreement).

The city banks lend primarily on a short-term basis; the long-term credit banks—namely, the Industrial Bank of Japan, the Long-Term Credit Bank of Japan, and the Nippon Credit Bank—were established under the Long-Term Credit Bank Law of 1952 for the purpose of lending long-term funds for capital investment. The long-term banks were formed in the early twentieth century as a semigovernmental organization to build up manufacturing industries. They were abolished during the period of Allied Occupation immediately following World War II. However, they were reintroduced due to the undeveloped state of long-term capital markets. The purpose of the new system was to draw a proper boundary line between long- and short-term financing so that the pressure for long-term financing on ordinary banks might be relieved.

The long-term credit banks' primary source of funds is bank debentures—five-year notes paying interest semiannually—and one-year discount notes. The issuance of bank debentures is a privilege given only to the long-term credit banks, with the exception of the Bank of Tokyo, another financial arm of the government established under the Foreign Exchange Bank Law, and Norin-Chukin Bank and Shoko-Chukin Bank. Such debentures represented 67.9 percent of the long-term credit banks' total liabilities and net worth in 1981. Long-term credit banks are authorized to issue debentures up to thirty times their combined total capital and reserves. They are not allowed to accept deposits from anybody but qualified clients, who are in many cases borrowers, and from the government. Lendings by long-term credit banks account for 10 percent of total lendings by all banks and 20 percent of total lendings for plant and equipment investments.

Debentures provide the bulk of the funding sources for long-term credit banks. Individual households are the largest single constituency of the bank debenture-holding group, with 49 percent of the total outstanding amount; the remaining half is widely dispersed among various private and public financial institutions. The significance of the bond holdings by other financial institutions and the government is that risks associated with long-term investments are also dispersed among them, with intermediation by the long-term banks.

The financing of long-term investments is also undertaken by the seven trust banks. Instead of issuing bank debentures, trust banks sell long-term trust certificates to the public and then lend their resources to finance plant expansions. The three long-term credit banks and the seven trust banks focus their lending activities on the financing of plant and equipment investments.

THE TRUST BANKS

Trust banks are major suppliers of long-term funds along with long-term credit banks. Trust accounts are one of the fastest growing areas in Japan's banking industry. In 1981 the total assets in trust accounts in the trust banks were 42.3 trillion yen, a figure equal to 32 percent of the city banks' total assets. Trust accounts grew at an annual compounded rate of 12.4 percent between 1975 and 1982. This rate exceeded city bank total assets' growth of 8.4 percent in the same period.

Under prevailing banking regulations, only ten institutions are permitted to operate in the trust business. These ten institutions include seven trust banks (namely, the Mitsubishi Trust & Banking Company, the Sumitomo Trust & Banking Company, the Mitsui Trust & Banking Company, the Yasuda Trust & Banking Company, the Toyo Trust & Banking Company, the Chuo Trust & Banking Company, and the Nippon Trust & Banking Company) and three ordinary banks (the Daiwa Bank, the Bank of Ryukyus, and the Okinawa Bank). Although the government and the Ministry of Finance planned to separate general banking and trust business completely in the post-World War II period, the Daiwa Bank showed a stubborn unwillingness to follow this government policy and has been allowed to operate as a trust bank. The Bank of Ryukyus and the Okinawa Bank are the legacy of the U.S. reign in the Ryukyu Islands until 1970. Although trust banks are allowed to engage in general banking activities, the trust business covers an overwhelmingly large share of their operations. Deposit banking accounts total only one-third of deposits in trust accounts.

Loans and discounts are by far the largest category on the asset side of trust banks' balance sheets. Borrowers of these funds are Japanese corporations, and funds are used mainly for plant and equipment expansions. These trust accounts supplied 8 percent of the total external fund requirements of Japanese industry in 1981. However, the trust banks' share of loans for new industrial equipments shrank from 12.7 percent in 1977 to 10.7 percent in 1981. On the other hand, the securities category increased sharply during the same period, with 19.3 percent of total assets in 1981, up from 9.1 percent, indicating the trust banks' increasingly active involvement in capital markets.

On the liability side, loan trust accounts represented nearly half of total liabilities, at 48.6 percent for the end of 1981. The Federation of Bankers Association of Japan indicates that individuals provide over 70 percent of loan trust contracts. Pension trusts, with 14.7 percent of total liabilities and net worth, was the next largest category after loan trust accounts. This category grew more rapidly than any other category with a compounded growth rate of 25.7 percent from 1977 to 1981.

CORPORATE FINANCIAL STRUCTURE

As mentioned earlier, Japanese firms meet their financial requirements by debt; more specifically, by borrowing from banks and not by issuing corporate debentures. As evidenced in Table 11-3, the long-term debt-to-debt equity ratio in Japanese firms is substantially higher than that of U.S. firms. The respective ratios stood at 104.4 percent versus 46.8 percent in 1979 (see Table 11-3). Their debt orientation is even more remarkable when total debt-to-equity ratios

Table 11-3. Ratio of Debt to Equity (%) for 256 U.S. and Japanese Manufacturing Corporations.

	1965	1970	1975	1979
Japan				
Long-term debt/equity	95.0	135.3	152.5	104.4
Total debt/equity	171.5	212.0	253.0	170.1
United States				
Long-term debt/equity	27.1	40.2	43.0	46.8
Total debt/equity	31.3	48.9	49.1	54.8

Source: Ministry of International Trade and Industry, *Sekai Kigyo Keiei Bunseki*, various years.

are examined by taking short-term debt into consideration. Japanese firms rely heavily on short-term as well as long-term debts. Their short-term debt-to-asset ratio fluctuated between 15 and 20 percent in the past twenty years as compared to ratios of 2.6 to 3.7 percent in U.S. firms. Japanese firms use short-term debt to meet a part of long-term requirements by continuously rolling it over at its maturity. Consequently, the difference between the two countries' use of debt versus equity becomes much wider: 170.1 percent for the Japanese and 54.6 percent for the Americans. This extensive use of short-term debt never caused a deterioration of Japanese firms' relationships with their banks because the firm's main bank is often a sister company and a shareholder.

SHAREHOLDERS

The majority of shares in Japanese firms are held primarily by institutions. Individuals do not account for a significant portion, representing only 28.5 percent of total shares of the firms that reported to the Association of National Stock Exchanges. The portion of individual shareholders is not only small but also decreasing constantly. Individuals accounted for 44.8 percent of total outstanding shares back in 1965. On the other hand, financial institutions, particularly banks, are rapidly increasing their share of stock ownership.

This phenomenon can be regarded as a recurrence of the *zaibatsu* system. The pre-World War II *zaibatsu*, most notably, Mitsubishi, Mitsui, and Yasuda, deployed companies in virtually all possible industries and tightly controlled them through a holding company which headed the group. On the top of the group was a large bank which helped finance the fund requirements of firms within the group. Groups also included a trading company, an insurance company, a petrochemical company, a metal company, and so forth. The system was somewhat like a conglomerate in the United States, but the size of each *zaibatsu* was much larger than a U.S. conglomerate, with just a handful of groups dominating Japanese industry. The alliance of *zaibatsu* firms is characterized by interlocking of directorates, with each firm owning some of the others' shares (Miyazaki 1973; Futatsugi 1973). The fact that a sizable portion of sales had been internally held must have contributed to the closed nature of the Japanese capital markets, as individuals and institutions were allowed only limited access to stock markets and information. After World War II the Allied Occupation tried to activate Japan's capital markets by opening stock markets to individuals. The portion of institutional shareholders was reduced to below 50 percent of total shares outstanding through dissolution efforts. Despite the Occupation's efforts, however, the groups remained. As of March 1981 the Sumitomo group topped all business groups by internally holding 26.1 percent of shares. Mitsubishi was a close second with 25.2 percent of shares.

In the context of increasing activity by institutional shareholders, financial institutions had the most notable growth, holding 37.3 percent of total shares outstanding in 1981, up from 23.3 percent in 1965. Shareholding by other domestic corporations (mostly manufacturing) has been stagnant since 1975 after a steady increase in the previous ten years. The ever-increasing holdings of financial institutions implies the importance of intragroup financing to Japanese industries. With intragroup financing, private firms can be less risk averse than if they relied totally on external capital markets to meet their fund requirements. Banks, on the other hand, have the benefit of maintaining certain customers (borrowers) in an environment of fierce competition within the Japanese banking industry. The Mitsubishi group led all the groups in terms of intragroup borrowing by fulfilling 24.9 percent of its requirements internally in 1981.

The institutional shareholding system also contributes to reduced dividend payments. The dividend payout ratio of Japanese firms is much lower than that of U.S. firms: 29.8 percent and 59.8 percent, respectively. Of the 1,438 firms listed on the Tokyo Stock Exchange, 254 pay no dividends at all. Japanese firms, therefore, retain a larger portion of net earnings internally to meet future funding requirements.

INDUSTRY VARIANCES

Comparisons of the samples of U.S. and Japanese corporations provide some insight into differences in financial conditions, policies, and performance in these two countries. Further examination at the industry level is also useful. For example, though the overall debt-to-equity ratio of Japanese industry is considerably higher than that of the U.S. industry, a closer look at individual industries indicates certain sectors have particularly high ratios (see Table 11-2). Steel and shipbuilding, for example, exhibit a debt-to-equity ratio of over 200 percent, even without considering short-term debt. Those Japanese industries with high long-term debt-to-equity ratios, of course, have a very small equity base (approximately 15 percent of total assets), while their U.S. counterparts maintained equity-to-total-asset ratios in the 50 percent range.

Compared to the above industries, most of which prospered in the early stage of Japan's economic growth, today's star category industries are maintaining relatively healthy financial conditions. Industries such as office and business machines, electrical machinery, household electronic apparatus, computer electronics, and automobile exhibit debt-equity ratios that range from 17.2 to 89 percent, as compared to a range of 22.8 to 45.3 percent among their U.S. counterparts. Two Japanese industries, namely automobile and household electronic apparatus, registered lower debt-to-equity ratios than their U.S. counterparts. The debt-to-equity ratio in these industries in Japan was 17.2 and 20.8 percent, respectively. The reason for the low ratios can be at least partially attributed to low dividend payment ratios. Household electronic apparatus and automobile's dividends in Japan were limited to a respective 21.5 and 19.4 percent of net earnings; their U.S. counterparts paid 37 and 68.4 percent in the same year. Dividend payment ratios were low throughout the sample of Japanese firms with an overall range of 30.9 percent as opposed to 74.5 percent for U.S. firms.

Another characteristic of Japanese balance sheets is a low current ratio. For the sample of major companies, the Japanese firms' current ratio was 112 percent and the U.S. firms' figure was 159 percent. The ratios for heavy industries were even lower. For example, the average current ratio of the four largest steel firms in Japan was 95.1 percent, indicating negative working capital.

It is widely believed that Japan's superb inventory control system reduces current assets and makes current ratios low. However, this may be a misleading statement. It is true that Japan's automobile industry has a much higher inventory turnover ratio (30.85), which is due to manufacturing centralization, product, component and supplies, rationalization, and the highly publicized *kanban* system. But this is an exception. For the seven industries presented in Table 11-2 the average Japanese firm's inventory turnover ratio is lower than that of their U.S. counterparts—6.33 versus 7.55. The steel industry in Japan, for example, recorded a lower turnover ratio than in the United States—4.35 versus 8.73. Lower inventory turnover ratios were also observed in some other industries for which Japan is famous, such as electronic machinery and computer electronics. The only finding in Japan's favor here is the inventory-to-asset ratio: 17.3 percent for Japan versus 19 percent for the United States.

The low current ratio observed in Japan is not due to lower inventory levels. It is due primarily to short-term debt. Short-term debt contributes to the large size of current liabilities, which reduces current ratios. If, hypothetically, we define that current liabilities do not include short-term debt, then the current ratio difference becomes much smaller. The ratio for Japan escalates to 157 percent, and the one for the United States is 182 percent. The current portion of long-term debt was another factor contributing to low current ratios. It accounted for nearly 20 percent of Japanese firms' assets, compared to only 10 percent of U.S. firms' assets. A Japanese firm's low current ratio should be ascribed not to slim current assets but to fat current liabilities.

Last, Japanese firms' asset turnover ratio is lower than that of U.S. firms: 1.10 versus 1.45. Is this because of Japanese firms' capital intensity? The answer is no. Japanese firms' property plant and equipment (PP&E) are working more efficiently than those of U.S. firms: the respective turnover ratios of PP&E to sales were 4.25 and 3.32 times. Instead, Japanese firms are carrying excessive liquid assets. Their ratio of current assets to sales was twice as high as that of U.S. firms. Particularly, a longer receivable collection period seems to be the major factor behind this distinction: 81.7 days for Japan as compared with 47.7 days for the U.S. firms. Also, investments in other companies due to the mutual shareholding system contribute to large noncurrent assets, pushing total fixed assets up.

The automobile industry seems to give an exception to every point. The turnover of PP&E was slower in Japan than in the United States, perhaps because of the Japanese automobile industry's heavy investments in advanced facilities. However, current asset turnover in the Japanese automobile industry was extremely high.

CONCLUSIONS

The most important contrast between U.S. and Japanese firms lies in their respective financial performance. Japanese firms realize rates of return significantly below those prevailing in the United States. This ability to operate with lower margins and returns represents a powerful competitive advantage for Japanese industry. The sources of that competitive advantage lie largely in the structure of Japanese capital markets and corporate finance. Group ownership ties and intragroup financing are important elements in this regard. More significantly, however, is the flow of funds within the broader economy. A high level of savings, stimulated in part by the low level of development in consumer finance options and the social security system, are funneled primarily into the postal savings system, the long-term credit banks, the trust banks, and the city banks (via rural and agricultural banks). The Japanese government exerts a high level of control, albeit indirect, over the use of these funds.

An immediate issue is the flow of funds out of Japan. The level of foreign lending activity has been small. Even in the recent past, with increased liberalization, Japanese foreign loans and investment are dwarfed by inflows (see Table 11-4). In addition to purchases of foreign bonds and stocks, Japanese banks can issue yen-denominated loans. Such loans are limited by a ceiling set by the Ministry of Finance. That ceiling was 1,300 trillion yen ($5.2 billion) for 1983 (*Japan Economic Journal* 1983).

Formal and informal restrictions on foreign yen-based lending contribute to the relatively low cost of capital in Japan. Low-cost capital permits Japanese firms to pursue long-term, capital-intensive strategies not available to their U.S. counterparts. This factor, rooted in the Japanese capital markets, provides Japanese industry with its greatest competitive advantage.

Table 11-4. Inflow and Outflow of Funds: April–May 1984.

	Purchase of Stocks and Bonds April–May 1984	
	Stocks	*Bonds*
Foreign investment in Japan	5,764	10,807
Japanese investment abroad	171	5,946

Source: Ministry of Finance, *Monthly Finance Review* (July 1984): 24–25.

APPENDIX 11A
Firms in the Sample of U.S. and Japanese Companies

U.S.A.

United States Steel Corp.
Bethlehem Steel Corp.
Armco Steel Corp.
National Steel Corp.
Republic Steel Corp.
Inland Steel Co.
Colt Industries Inc.
Allegheny Ludlum Ind. Inc.
Cyclops Corp.
Sundstrand
Cincinnati Milacron Inc.
Ex-Cell-O Corp.
International Harvester Co.
Caterpillar Tractor Co.
Deere & Co.
FMC Corp.
Dresser Ind., Inc.
Ingersoll-Rand Co.
Xerox Corp.
Minnesota Mining & Manufacturing Co.
Burroughs Corp.
The Singer Co.
The Timken Co.
Federal-Mogul Corp.
General Electric Co.
Westinghouse Electric Corp.
North American Phillips Corp.
Whirlpool Corp.
Emerson Electric Co.
Motorola Inc.
Gould Inc.
McGraw-Edison Co.
International Telephone & Telegraph Co.
General Telephone & Electronics Corp.
RCA Corporation
Sperry Rand Corp.
International Business Machines Corp.
NCR Corp.
Control Data Corp.

Digital Equipment Corp.
LTV Corp.
Litton Ind., Inc.
Honeywell Inc.
Raytheon Co.
Teledyne Inc.
Texas Instrument Inc.
Hewlett Packard Co.
Dun & Bradstreet Inc.
Computer Sciences Corp.
Automatic Data Processing Inc.
Planning Research Corp.
General Motors Corp.
Ford Motor Co.
Chrysler Corp.
Bendix Corp.
TRW Inc.
Borg-Warner Corp.
Eaton Corp.
Fruehauf Corp.
Dana Corp.
Clark Equipment Corp.
Rockwell International Corp.
United Technologies Corp.
Boeing Co.
McDonnell Douglas Corp.
Lockheed Aircraft Corp.
General Dynamics Corp.
Todd Shipyards Corp.
American Ship Building Co.
Polaroid Corp.
Bell & Howell Co.
E. I. Du Pont de Nemours & Co.
Union Carbide Corp.
The Dow Chemical Co.
Monsanto Co.
W. R. Grace & Co.
Allied Chemical Corp.
American Cyanimid Co.

U.S.A. (continued)

Eastman Kodak Co.
Johnson & Johnson
American Home Products Corp.
Warner-Lambert Co.
Bristol-Myers Co.
Pfizer, Inc.
Merck & Co., Inc.
Dart Industries Inc.
The Procter & Gamble Co.
Colgate-Palmolive Co.
Avon Products Inc.
Revlon Inc.
Chesebrough Ponds Inc.
Owens-Illinois Inc.
PPG Ind., Inc.
Corning Glass Works
Lone Star Industries, Inc.
Ideal Basic Ind., Inc.
Goodyear Tire & Rubber Co.
The Firestone Tire & Rubber Co.
Uniroyal Inc.
The General Tire & Rubber Co.
The B.F. Goodrich Co.
Burlington Ind., Inc.
Levi Strauss
United Merchants Manufactures
West Point Pepperell Inc.
Cone Mills Corp.
Dan River Inc.
Cannon Mills Co.
Celanese Corp.
J.P. Stevens & Co., Inc.
Spring Mills Inc.
International Paper Co.
Georgia-Pacific Corp.
Weyerhaeuser Co.
Crown Zellerbach Corp.
St. Regis Paper Co.
The Mead Corp.
Kimberly-Clark Corp.
Scott Paper Co.
Union Camp Corp.

Exxon Corp.
Texaco Inc.
Mobil Oil Corp.
Standard Oil Co. of California
Gulf Oil Corp.
Standard Oil Co. (An Indiana Corp.)
Shell Oil Co.
Atlantic Richfield Co.
Conoco Inc.
Aluminium Co. of America
Reynolds Metals Co.
Kaiser Aluminium & Chemical Corp.
Kennecott Copper Corp.
G.K. Technologies Inc.
AMAX Inc.
Asarco Inc.
Phelps Dodge Corp.
Pittston Co.
Eastern Gas & Fuel Associates
Kraft Inc.
Borden Inc.
Carnation Co.
The Coca-Cola Co.
Pepsico Inc.
Nabisco Inc.
Hershey-Foods Corp.
Esmark Inc.
Beatrice Foods Co.
General Foods Corp.
Consolidated Foods Corp.
CPC International Inc.
Armour & Co.
General Mills Inc.
H.J. Heinz Co.
AMF Inc.
Brunswick Corp.
Interco Inc.
Melville Corp.
GENESCO Inc.
Brown Group Inc.
United States Shoe Corp.

Japan

Shinnion Iron & Steel Co., Ltd.
Nippon Kokan Co., Ltd.
Sumitomo-Metal Industries, Ltd.
Kawasaki Steel Corp.
Daido Special Steel Co., Ltd.
Hitachi Metals Ltd.
Aichi Steel Works Ltd.
Toshiba Machine Co., Ltd.
Toyoda Machine Works, Ltd.
Makino Milling Machine Co., Ltd.
Kubota Ltd.
Komatsu Mfg. Co., Ltd.
Ricoh Co., Ltd.
Casio Computer Co., Ltd.
Tokyo Electric Co., Ltd.
Brother Ind., Ltd.
Janome Sewing Machine Co., Ltd.
Riccar Sewing Machine Co., Ltd.
Nippon Seiko Co., Ltd.
Koyo Seiko Co., Ltd.
The Toyo Bearing Mfg., Co., Ltd.
Hitachi Ltd.
Tokyo Shibaura Electric Co., Ltd.
Mitsubishi Electric Corp.
Matsushita Electric Inc. Co., Ltd.
Sanyo Electric Co., Ltd.
Sony Corp.
Sharp Corp.
Nippon Electric Co., Ltd.
Oki Electric Industry Co., Ltd.
Fujitsu Ltd.
TDK Electronics Co., Ltd.
Alps Electric Co., Ltd.
Yokokawa Electric Works Ltd.
Toyota Motor Co., Ltd.
Nissan Motor Co., Ltd.
Nippon Denso Co., Ltd.
NHK Spring Co., Ltd.
Kayaba Ind. Co., Ltd.
Mitsubishi Heavy Ind., Ltd.
Ishikwajima-Harima Heavy Inc. Co., Ltd.
Kawasaki Heavy Ind., Ltd.
Cannon Camera Co., Inc.

Nippon Kogaku Co., Ltd.
Minolta Camera Co., Ltd.
Olympus Optical Co., Ltd.
Mitsubishi Chemical Inc. Ltd.
Sumitomo Chemical Co., Ltd.
Fuji Photo Film Co., Ltd.
Konishiroku Photo Ind. Co., Ltd.
Takeda Chemical Ind., Ltd.
Shionogi & Co., Ltd.
Sankyo Co., Ltd.
Shiseido Co., Ltd.
Kao Soap Co., Ltd.
The Lion Co., Ltd.
Asahi Glass Co., Ltd.
Nippon Sheet Glass Co., Ltd.
Mitsubishi Mining & Cement Co., Ltd.
Onoda Cement Co., Ltd.
Nippon Cement Co., Ltd.
Bridgestone Tire Co., Ltd.
The Yokohama Rubber Co., Ltd.
Kurabo Industries Ltd.
Nisshin Spinning Co., Ltd.
Nitto Boseki Co., Ltd.
Asahi Chemical Ind. Co., Ltd.
Tore Co., Ltd.
Teijin Ltd.
The Japan Wool Textile Co., Ltd.
The Wool Spinning & Weaving Co., Ltd.
Daito Woolen Spinning & Weaving Co., Ltd.
Jujo Paper Mfg. Co., Ltd.
Oji Paper Co., Ltd.
Sanyo Kokusaku Pulp Co., Ltd.
Nippon Oil Co., Ltd.
Maruzen Oil Co., Ltd.
Nippon Light Metal Co., Ltd.
The Furukawa Electric Co., Ltd.
Sumitomo Electric Ind. Ltd.
Mitsubishi Metal Mining Co., Ltd.
Mitsui Mining & Smelting Co., Ltd.
Sumitomo Metal Mining Co., Ltd.
Mitsui Mining Co., Ltd.
Snow Brand Milk Products Co., Ltd.
Meiji Milk Products Co., Ltd.

Japan (*continued*)

Morinaga Milk Ind. Co., Ltd.	Ajinomoto Co., Inc.
The Calpis Food Ind. Co., Ltd.	Nisshin Flour Milling Co., Ltd.
Meiji Seika Kaisha, Ltd.	R. K. Mizuno Co., Ltd.
Morinaga Confectionery Co., Ltd.	Chiyoda Shoes Co., Ltd.
Taiyo Fisher Co., Ltd.	

REFERENCES

Bank of Japan. 1971-1982. *Economic Statistics Annual*.

———. Various years. "Short-Term Economic Survey of Principal Enterprises."

Futatsugi, Yusaku. 1973. "The Measurement of Interfirm Relationships." *Japanese Economic Studies* (Fall): 62-89.

Japan Economic Journal. 1983. April 26: 3.

Ministry of Finance. 1984. *Monthly Finance Review* (July): 24-25.

Ministry of International Trade and Industry (MITI). 1982. *Sekai Kigyo no Keiei Bunseki*.

Miyazaki, Yoshikazu. 1973. "The Japanese-Type Structure of Big Business." *Japanese Economic Studies* (Fall): 3-60.

12 JAPANESE CORPORATE FINANCE AND CORPORATE CAPITAL STRUCTURE

Takuro Isoda

This chapter traces the evolution of corporate finance methods in the Japanese economy after World War II to the present and offers some projections on future trends among Japanese firms. It then proceeds to examine the capital market structure primarily in terms of its implications for the management and investment of corporate funds in Japanese companies.

CORPORATE FINANCE METHODS

For two decades preceding the first oil crisis in 1973-1974, the Japanese economy enjoyed an average annual growth rate in excess of 10 percent. Under such favorable economic conditions Japanese corporations did not have to be overly concerned about financing costs for expansion, as expected and actual returns on investments in equipment and inventories almost always exceeded their costs. At that time the major concern of corporations was to obtain sufficient money to finance their expansion needs. Figure 12-1 shows the relationship between recurring profit and equity ratio in large Japanese manufacturing companies with paid-in capital of at least 1 billion yen (approximately $42 million) over the time period 1966 to 1982.

After the 1973-1974 oil crisis, however, the Japanese economy entered a stage of moderate but steady growth. The rate of growth

152 STRATEGIC MANAGEMENT IN THE FINANCIAL SECTOR

Figure 12-1. Comparison of Interest Rate (payment) and Return on Assets.

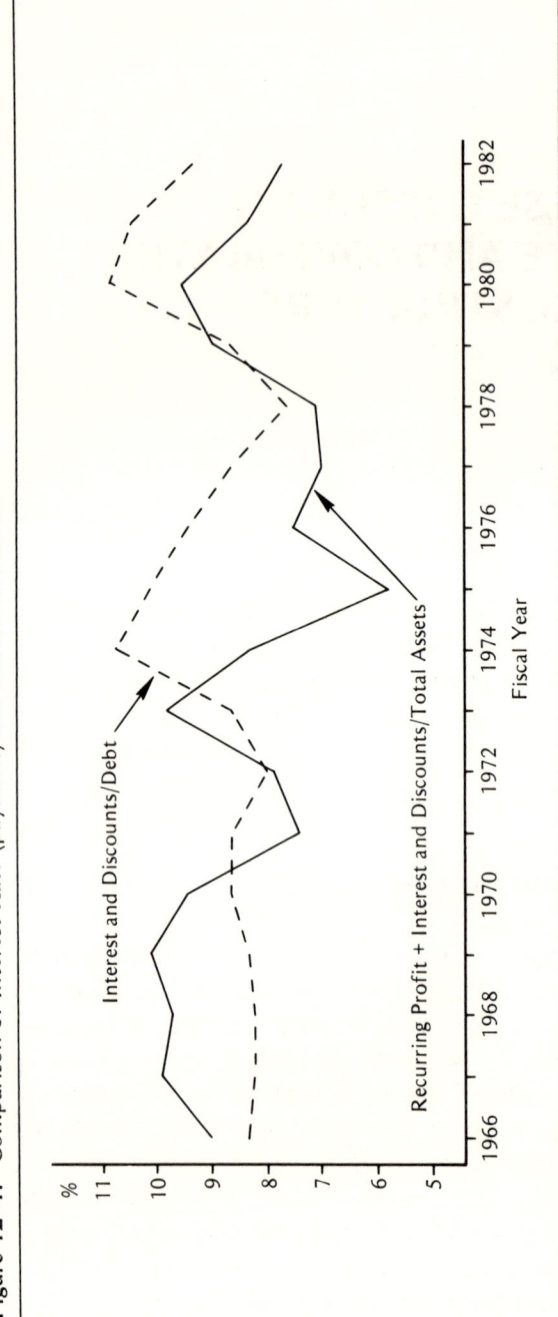

Note: Relationship between the recurring profit and the Equity Ratio in large manufacturing companies.

m: recurring profit/equity
i: interest and discounts/debt
r: recurring profit + interest and discounts/total assets
D: debt E: equity

$$mE = r(E+D) - iD$$

recurring profit = recurring profit + Interest and discounts received − interest and discounts paid

$$m = r + (r-i)\frac{D}{E}.$$

Therefore, when i is larger than r, for m to increase, $\frac{D}{E}$ must decrease (besides, if the equity ratio is $\frac{E}{E+D}$, then the decrease of $\frac{D}{E}$ means an increase in the equity ratio).

in corporate earnings decelerated and in some cases even reversed. At the same time, worldwide interst rates increased. As a result of excess production capacity, which was caused by capital investments made prior to the oil crisis, corporations slowed their expansion plans and investments in equipment. This set into motion a chain of events. Because of slower growth, tax revenues decreased substantially—so much so that in 1975 the Japanese government was compelled to adopt a deficit budget policy. To finance the deficit a series of sizable government bond issues was floated. This pushed up domestic interest rates.

Consequently, the oil crisis caused a fundamental change in the way Japanese corporate treasurers had to meet their funding needs. Prior to the crisis their first priority was to maintain a smooth pipeline of money from the banks. After the crisis and its accompanying changes in the economic climate, companies increasingly sought to finance their capital needs through internally generated funds as much as possible.

The oil crisis marked a significant turning point in the methods of corporate financing in Japan. From then onward, Japanese corporations began to concentrate on minimizing financing costs and maximizing income from cash liquidity.

Shift from Bank Borrowings to Capital Market Financing

As previously stated, before the oil crisis the primary objective of Japanese corporations was to maintain sources of funds to sustain rapid growth. Most of the external funds were borrowed from commercial banks. Consequently, Japanese companies were very highly leveraged. After the oil crisis major corporations began to shift gradually and are still continuing to shift their method of external financing from one of debt financing (primarily short-term bank loans) to that of equity financing, such as issues of common stock and convertible bonds.

The preference for equity financing also stemmed from the fact that the Japanese corporate treasurer considered the cost of debt to be higher than that of common stock. His measuring stick was based strictly on dividends as a percentage of par rather than required return on equity.

Table 12-1. Ways of Financing: Large Companies.[a]

(billion yen, %)

	1973-1974 Period of Tight Money	1975-1978 Period of Easy Money	1979 Period of Tight Money	1980-1982 Period of Easy Money
External financing	10 367 (68.8)	5 701 (51.2)	7 667 (50.4)	9 051 (49.0)
Capital stock	973 (6.5)	1 386 (12.5)	1 222 (8.0)	2 223 (12.0)
Bonds	666 (4.4)	924 (8.3)	1 381 (9.1)	865 (4.7)
Long-term debt	3 651 (24.2)	1 321 (11.9)	701 (4.6)	2 814 (15.2)
Short-term debt	5 077 (33.7)	2 071 (18.6)	4 363 (28.7)	3 150 (17.1)
Internal financing	4 711 (31.2)	5 425 (48.8)	7 554 (49.6)	9 416 (51.0)
Total financing (external + internal)	15 078 (100.0)	11 126 (100.0)	15 221 (100.0)	18 467 (100.0)
Total demand of funds	17 206	10 125	16 109	18 159

a. A large company is one with capital stock of more than one billion yen.
Note: 1. Figures are averaged yearly for each period.
  2. Figures within parentheses: breakdown.
Source: Ministry of Finance figures, various years.

Prior to 1969 Japanese corporations had traditionally offered new shares at par value and allocated them to existing shareholders. However, they slowly changed their method of capital increases from the par value basis to the market price basis. By offering shares at market value to both existing and new shareholders, Japanese corporations were able to raise more funds and narrow the price differential between the primary and secondary markets. Capital increases using the market price basis accounted for 86.7 percent of all new equity financing in 1983, as compared to an average of 62.9 percent during the period 1975 to 1979 and 49 percent in 1973.

Other types of equity financing, such as convertible debentures and warrants, also became popular. Convertible debentures represented 62.4 percent of all bond issues in 1983, as compared to an average of 25.6 percent during the years 1975 to 1979.

In summary, since the 1973-1974 oil crisis two major trends in Japanese financing emerged. One, the shift from bank borrowings to capital market financing, with a concomitant move from bonds issued with mortgages to unsecured bonds. Two, an emphasis on equity financing rather than debt.

Utilization of Overseas Markets

Another significant trend in methods of financing is the increasing use of overseas markets. With the amendment to the Foreign Exchange Law issued at the end of 1980, regulations for borrowings of foreign bank loans were eased and issuance of foreign-currency-denominated bonds was largely deregulated. This increased the corporations' ability to utilize foreign money. Table 12-2 shows the diversification of external financing in large Japanese corporations for the years 1970 to 1983. In 1983 financing in foreign currencies as a percentage of total external financing was 45.3 percent. This compared to a mere 1.3 percent during the time period 1970 to 1974.

Of all the available overseas capital markets, the Swiss franc market was the most popular. In 1983, for example, Swiss franc issues accounted for 73.8 percent of all overseas bond issues by Japanese corporations. In total, foreign-currency-denominated corporate bond issues (mainly convertible debentures) amounted to $7.6 billion in 1983, which was higher than the total corporate bonds launched domestically during the same year ($6.2 billion). In the same year thirteen corporations not listed on any stock exchange also floated their bonds abroad in the total amount of $122 million. Table 12-3 presents the findings of a questionnaire survey conducted by the Bonds and Debenture Underwriting Association to determine the motives of Japanese corporations in issuing foreign currency bonds.

The advantages associated with the timely utilization of overseas markets are primarily threefold: One, lower costs, primarily because of a relatively strong Japanese yen vis-à-vis the various European currencies. Two, the need to hedge against foreign exchange risks re-

Table 12-2. Diversification of External Financing in Large Japanese Corporations, All Industries.

	1970-1974 Average	1975-1979 Average	1980-1983 Average	1981	1982	1983
Total external financing	100.0%	100.0%	100.0%	100.0%	100.0%	100.0%
Loans	83.9	63.8	64.7	69.0	63.1	45.4
Yen loans	82.5	60.7	51.1	54.5	50.0	24.4
Impact loans[a]	1.4	3.1	13.6	14.5	13.1	21.0
Bonds	5.9	17.7	11.4	6.9	14.7	21.9
Domestic	6.0	13.7	3.8	4.2	4.7	-1.0
Overseas	-0.1	4.0	7.6	2.7	10.0	22.9
Stocks[b]	10.2	18.5	23.9	24.1	22.2	32.7
Domestic	10.2	17.9	22.4	22.2	20.8	31.2
Depository receipt	-0.0	0.6	1.5	1.9	1.4	1.5
Financing in yen	98.7	92.2	77.3	80.9	75.5	54.7
Financing in foreign currencies	1.3	7.8	22.7	19.1	24.5	45.3

a. Impact loans are loans with no limitation on the purpose or usage of funds.
b. Stocks include those converted from convertible bonds.
Note: Breakdown of loans, bonds, and stocks are estimated by sources of the Ministry of Finance and others.
Source: Ministry of Finance figures, various years.

Table 12-3. Questionnaire Survey on Motives for Issuing Bonds in Foreign Currencies.[a]

	(Breakdown: %)
Diversification of financing	88.3
Lower cost	82.5
Unnecessary for secured mortgages	33.9
Easier procedure for issuing	29.2
Expectation to be better known overseas	21.6
Necessary for foreign currencies (including hedging against foreign exchange risks)	14.6
Issuing conditions reflect company results	5.3
Allocation for repayment of bonds in foreign currencies	1.8
Others	1.2
Total	100.0

a. Answers from 171 companies; includes duplicate answers.
Source: Bonds and Debentures Underwriting Association, "The Questionnaire Survey on Issuing Bonds," May 1983.

sulting from increasing overseas investments. Three, easier and more flexible financing procedures in major European and Asian capital markets, particularly the Swiss franc issue market.

New Developments

Looking into the future it is possible to identify several emerging trends.

Increasingly Sophisticated Funding Operations. Because of the policy of administrative guidance by the Japanese government and the powerful influence of the major Japanese banks, corporate financing techniques have been limited. Corporate funding strategies, however, are becoming increasingly sophisticated. Through careful monitoring of interest rate differentials and exchange rate fluctuations between the world's major currencies, Japanese corporations have not hesitated to become more involved in foreign currency borrowings combined with currency and interest rate swaps. Japanese banks, which lend to the larger corporations, have grown slowly in recent years but now appear eager to assist them by providing swap facilities.

Table 12-4. Companywide Breakdown of Borrowings by National Banks (*percentage increase versus year earlier*).

	End of Dec. 1981	End of Dec. 1982	End of Dec. 1983	End of Mar. 1984
Borrowings By:				
Large companies	8.8	8.5	6.8	4.2
Small and medium companies	8.6	11.8	14.8	15.9

Source: Bank of Japan figures, various years.

Table 12-4 shows a breakdown of borrowings by large vis-à-vis small to medium-sized companies.

Independence of Foreign Subsidiaries and Centralization of Finance/Accounting Functions. The overseas subsidiaries of Japanese corporations are growing more independent of their parent companies for funding transactions. In addition to bank loans, bond issues, and commercial paper issues, their parent companies have encouraged them to make the utmost use of local facilities, such as industrial revenue bond (IRB) issues in the United States. Domestically, however, parent companies tend to involve themselves more in their subsidiaries' financial transactions. With the support of advanced computer technology, in some cases the asset/liability management for both the parent company and its subsidiaries are centralized and handled by a finance and accounting subsidiary operated by the parent company. This can be called the "new group finance management" concept.

Acquisitions. Acquisition of other corporations or businesses, instead of making investments in new plants and equipment, is still the exception rather than the rule in Japan. Acquisitions, which were historically unpopular in Japan, usually occur only in cases where the acquired company is suffering serious financial difficulty. A new development, however, is the acquisition of overseas companies by Japanese corporations.

Others. Since the investment tax-exempt system does not exist in Japan, lease terms offered by lease companies remain less attractive to corporations. Large corporations seldom use lease contracts because the former's financial cost for investments is lower than that of the lease companies. Shipping and airline companies, however, often seek sale/lease-back contracts wherein they can deduct a larger amount of expenses over a shorter time span, as much as 30 percent of depreciation period regulated by tax laws. For example, if the regulated period for depreciation were ten years, they could depreciate it in three years or longer.

MANAGING AND INVESTING CORPORATE FUNDS

This section examines the capital market structure in Japan, primarily in terms of its implications for the management and investment of corporate funds.

Importance of Recurring Profit

Japanese corporations may appear to be less experienced than their U.S. counterparts in the management of financial operations. This is partly the consequence of various regulations they had to follow and also partly the result of an inherited business philosophy that money must be made from their own business. Given this background, corporations always placed primary importance on increasing operating profit. Securities analysts in Japan are apt to give a better credit rating to companies the operating profits of which grow constantly and quickly.

Of the three major methods of measuring profitability—net present value, payback period, and return on investment—the payback period method has been the most popular and the net present value method the least popular. This is largely a function of the fact that during the past several decades Japanese corporations have financed their investments through bank borrowings. In order to qualify for bank loans the proposed investment had to be sufficiently profitable to pay back total debt and interest within a certain time period.

Table 12-5. Change of Equity Ratio: Large Companies.[a]

Fiscal[b]	Manufacturers	Materials	Assembly	Nonmanufacturers
		(%)		
1966	27.1	26.3	28.1	20.3
1969	24.6	23.8	25.5	17.7
1974	19.9	17.4	23.1	12.8
1975	18.5	15.6	22.3	12.6
1976	18.4	15.0	22.8	12.3
1977	19.3	15.2	24.2	13.2
1978	20.4	16.0	25.6	13.7
1979	20.6	15.7	26.5	12.5
1980	21.8	16.5	27.9	13.4
1981	22.7	16.4	29.7	13.6
1982	24.1	17.4	31.3	13.4

a. A large company is one with capital stock of more than one billion yen.
b. Equity figures before 1981 include the specified estimated liabilities a/c which were abolished by the amendment of the Commercial Law Act in October 1982.

Note: Equity ratio = $\dfrac{\text{equity}}{\text{(total assets (debt + equity))}}$.

Source: Bank of Japan figures, various years.

Capital Structure

This emphasis on profitability also had its implications for capital structure. Traditionally, Japanese corporations were very profitable but also highly leveraged. This situation changed after the oil crisis, when recurring profits declined and equity increased due to the shift from bank borrowings to equity financing.

As a result of this shift, the net worth ratio, which had been deteriorating during the era of high economic growth, started to improve constantly although raw material producers and the nonmanufacturing sectors have not yet shown any significant improvement. See Table 12-5.

While processed goods manufacturers experienced only a momentary impact from the second oil crisis, raw material manufacturers required more time to recover. This delay in improvement in the nonmanufacturing sector primarily reflects the continued large in-

Figure 12-2. Relationship between Recurring Profit/Equity and Stockholders' Equity Ratio (*manufacturers*).

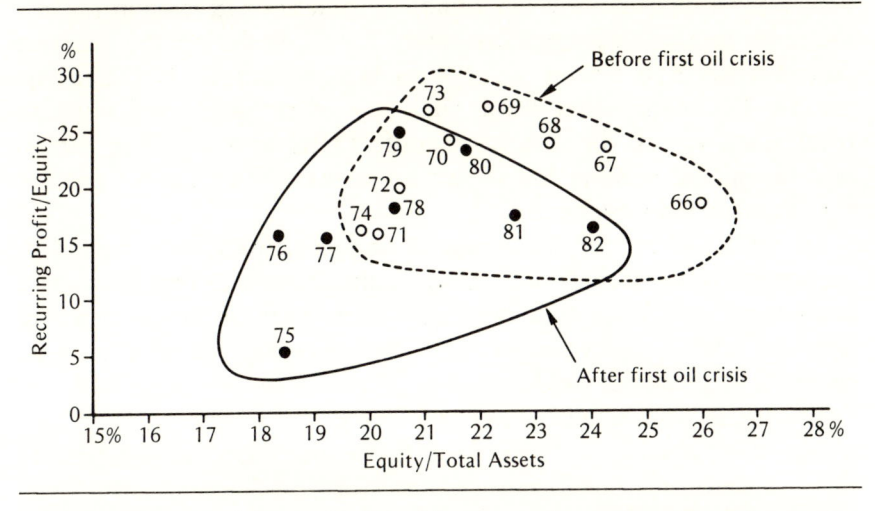

Note: Open circles (o) and solid circles (●) represent the percentage figures for recurring profit against equity.
Source: Bank of Japan.

vestments by electric utilities which are still heavily dependent on external financing.

An interesting point is that the ratio of operating profit to sales improved in tandem with the recovery in net worth ratio after the first oil crisis, whereas a lower net worth ratio and higher operating profit ratio were observed before the crisis. See Figure 12-2.

With greater equity and slower growth, liquidity began to increase. As a result, Japanese corporations had to pay more attention to cash management. Financial experts, once subordinate to marketing people among management, now gained an equal chance to join the corporate executive team.

Liquidity

With slower growth it was natural for corporations to devote serious attention to improving financial income as they struggled to minimize financial costs. After the oil crisis when the Japanese economy again entered into a period of steady growth, liquidity started to increase and, in fact, grew so large that it was not possible simply to deposit it with banks. Among corporations having a paid-in capital of 1 billion yen (U.S. $42 million),—about 1,800 corporations or 0.1 percent of approximately 1.8 million corporations existing in Japan—the total retained earnings increased 2.8 times during the ten-year period, from $58 billion in 1974 to $162 billion in 1983. See Figure 12-3. On the other hand, the ratio of tangible fixed assets to total assets for all the nation's manufacturers with a paid-in capital of $42 million or more has shown an increase of a mere 0.8 percent for the same ten-year period.

In 1975, when corporate accounting principles were amended, corporations began to disclose their financial assets in two categories: short-term and long-term holdings. Short-term securities refer to holdings within one year. In 1976 the percentage of long- vis-à-vis short-term securities holdings of large manufacturers with $42 million or more paid-in capital were 6.3 percent and 3.1 percent of total assets, respectively. In 1983 these figures increased to 7.2 percent and 4.8 percent, respectively. Adding cash and deposits of 11.7 percent, total financial assets were as much as 23.7 percent of total assets in 1983, which is quite close to the figure of total tangible fixed assets.

In 1983 eleven Japanese corporations had short-term liquidity exceeding $1 billion. Of these, six corporations held over $2 billion. Financial asset management varies from corporation to corporation. For example, in 1983 Toyota Motor, the most cash-rich company in Japan, divided its total financial assets of $5.4 billion into short-term holdings of 59 percent and long-term holdings of 41 percent. In contrast, Matsushita Electric Industrial allocated $3.8 billion (or 98 percent of its financial assets) to long-term holdings, primarily consisting of long-term bonds and bank deposits. These differences across corporations do not stem from the industry structure per se, but rather from the different investment policies of the respective companies. On the whole, available short-term liquidity of Japanese corporations increased by $11 billion during 1983 to reach $53 billion.

In the past the major task of financial officers in Japanese corporations was to maintain intimate relationships with banks. Planning for plant and equipment investments was first and foremost; financing followed. Now, the management of cash flow and accumulation of financial assets in Japan are not merely for the purpose of financ-

Figure 12-3. Increase of Real Retained Earnings: All Industries, Capital Stock More Than 1 Billion Yen.[a]

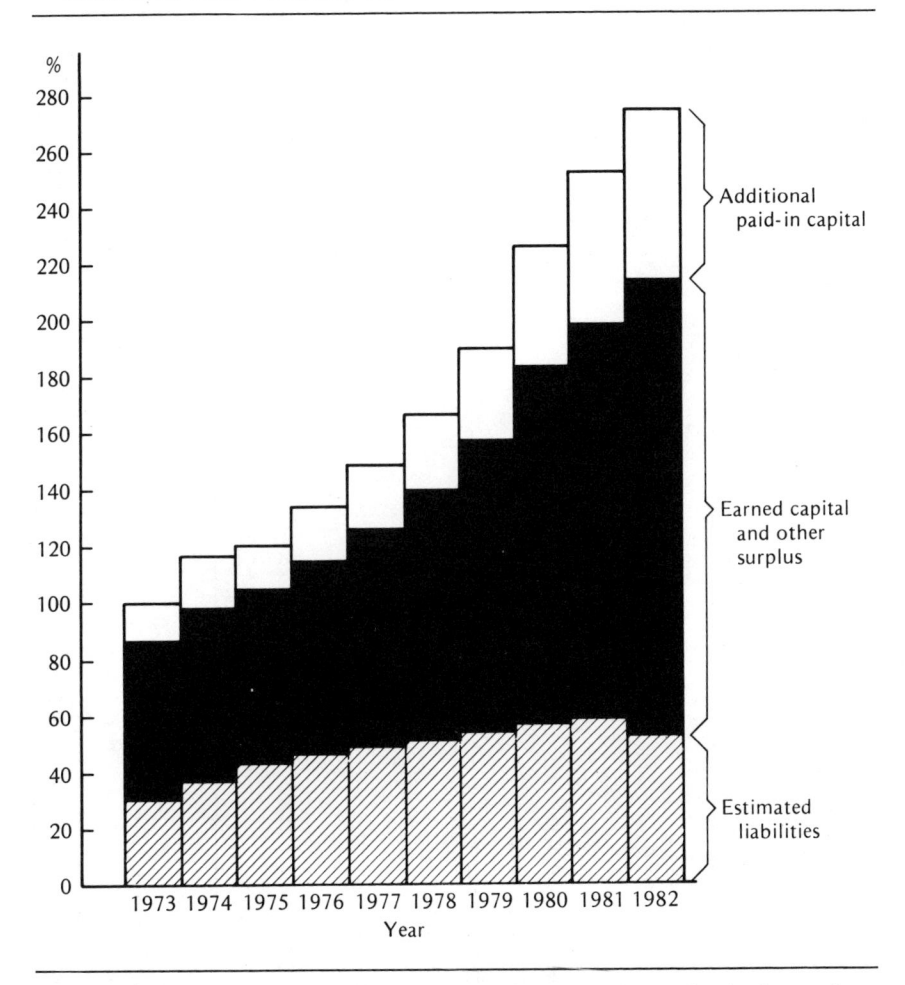

a. Real retained earnings = additional paid-in capital + earned capital and other surplus + long-term estimated liabilities + specified liabilities.
Note: 1973 Real retained earnings, 14 trillion yen = 100.
Source: Adapted from Ministry of Finance statistics, 1983.

Table 12-6. Uses of Funds in Large Companies, All Industries (*breakdown: %*).

	1970-1974 Average	1975-1979 Average	1980-1982 Average	1981	1982	1983
Total increase of funds	100.0	100.0	100.0	100.0	100.0	100.0
Cash and deposits	61.1	40.4	50.6	58.9	42.0	34.6
CD[a]	—	3.9	13.4	12.4	11.0	18.5
Deposits in foreign currencies[b]	2.2	0.9	21.9	9.2	22.7	34.1
Securities held for short term[c]	6.7	36.3	14.6	8.2	16.4	33.4
Securities held for long term[d]	32.2	23.3	34.8	32.9	41.6	32.0
Used for interest-regulated financial products[e]	59.0	35.5	15.3	37.3	8.2	-18.0
Used for non-interest-regulated financial products[f]	12.1	35.0	50.2	30.8	47.2	85.8
Used for stocks	28.9	29.5	34.5	31.9	44.6	32.2
Used for foreign currencies	2.8	2.4	29.9	14.1	31.4	47.8

a. Estimated.
b. Estimated.
c. Securities held for short term = securities a/c in current assets of B/S.
d. Securities held for long term = securities a/c in fixed assets of B/S.
e. Used for interest-regulated financial products = cash and deposits − CD − deposits in foreign currencies.
f. Used for non-interest-regulated financial products = bonds and debentures + CD + deposits in foreign currencies.

Sources: Ministry of Finance figures, various years; Bank of Japan figures, various years.

ing production facilities, as in the case of other countries. Often, financial officers look for the cheapest money, either domestically or abroad, to reinvest it everywhere to create additional financial profit.

Short- and Long-Term Money Market Instruments

In Japan interest rates for bank deposits in yen are traditionally regulated. In the past decade, however, more unregulated money market instruments have been made available to investors, including corporations. Table 12-6 presents the changing trend in the uses of funds in large companies over the period 1970 to 1983.

Introduced in 1975, *gensaki* (or the purchase of bonds with resale agreement) was the most popular money market instrument for a few years. After 1978 certificates of deposit (CDs) and foreign currency deposits, which were liberalized in 1980, have shown a steady increase. The combined outstanding amount of *gensaki*, foreign currency deposits, and CD holdings reached $53.8 billion in 1984. Most notable, however, has been the upswing of foreign currency deposits and foreign bonds, which absorbed 47.8 percent of all newly added liquidity during 1983. Foreign bonds were purchased initially by trading firms and oil refinery companies to hedge against foreign exchange risks for their foreign currency debts. Now, corporations that do not engage in business involving foreign currencies are also investing in foreign bonds. In 1983 total outstanding investments in foreign bonds by Japanese corporations were estimated at $6.5 billion or 13 percent of total foreign bond investments in Japan. Foreign-currency-denominated CDs and commercial paper were also introduced in April 1984. After six months total holdings by corporations were estimated at $4 billion.

In light of all of the aforementioned changes in capital structure, it should not be long before nonoperating or financial profit will play as important a role as operating profit in Japanese corporate financial management.

INDEX

Abbott Co., 108, 110
Acquisition, 72, 112, 121, 122, 158
Administrative guidance, 11-13, 19, 24, 26, 157
 See also industrial policy, industrial targeting
Aerospace industry, xxii, 27, 87-97
Agricultural sector, 8, 28, 67
Airbus, 87
Airline companies, 16, 159
 See also aerospace industry and Boeing Commercial Airplane Co.
Alfa-Laval, 73, 74
All Nippon Airlines, 88
Allied Occupation, 8, 25, 139, 143
Aluminum industry, 11, 48
American Chamber of Commerce, 27
American Home Products, 105, 108, 148
American Revolution, 25
Antibiotics, 99, 109, 110, 114
Apple Computer, 125
Aoyama Gakuin University, xx
Asano Portland Cement Co., 24
Association of National Stock Exchanges, 142
Astronet, 50
Automobile industry, xxii, 12, 18, 19, 37, 38, 58, 90, 94-96, 117, 118, 120, 123, 144, 145

Bacher, Thomas, xxii, 87
Ballon, Robert, xix, xx, 3
Banks, commercial, 11, 30, 35, 36
 city, 34, 138-140, 146, 157
 foreign, 24
 internationalization of, 34-36, 44
 trust, 140, 141, 146
Bank of Japan, 138
Bank of Ryukyus, 140
Bank of Tokyo, 34, 35, 139
Bankruptcy, 116
Banyu, xxiv, 111, 112
Battelle Memorial Institute, 50
Bechtel, 38
Beecham, 107, 108
Beverage industry, 76
"Big Nine" general trading companies, 36, 41, 45
Biotechnology, 62, 95
Boeing Commercial Airplane Co., xxii, 87-97, 147
Boeing-CTDC venture, xxii, xxiv, 87-97
Bonds and Debenture Underwriting Association, 155, 157
Brazil, 49
Bribery, 40, 41, 87
Bridgestone Tire Co., 121, 149
Bristol-Myers Co., 105, 106, 108, 148
Bureaucracy, 4, 5, 13, 14, 25

167

INDEX

Buy-back, 48
Business International, xxi, 66, 67, 69, 71, 74, 77, 79, 81

Camera industry, 95, 96, 120
Capital market structure, 133–146, 151–165
Cartel arrangements, 116
Certificate of deposits, 165
Charter statements, 73–75
Chemical industry, 11, 56, 70
China, 25
Chino, 51
Chuo Trust and Banking Co., 140
Ciba Geigy, 105–108, 111
C. Itoh, 38
Civil service, 6, 9, 13, 18
Civil Transport Development Corp., xxii, 88, 89, 94
Clans, 23, 24
Clinical data, 100, 101
Clinoril, 111
Codevelopment, xxiii, 111–113
Collaborative/cooperative agreements, xxiii, xxiv, 88–97
  See also codevelopment, comarketing, countertrade, joint ventures, licensing
Columbia University, xx
Comarketing, xxiii, 111–113
Communication problems, 30, 41, 124, 125
Commission fee, 36, 59, 68, 72, 80, 82, 83
Competitive spirit, 26, 116, 117
Computer industry, xxii, 11, 12, 30, 49, 94–96, 125, 144, 145
Confucianism, 6, 26
Consensus building, 12–14, 17–20
Consultation Committees, 10, 14, 20
Cost center, 76–79, 81
Counterpurchase, 48
Countertrade, xxi, xxii, 39, 47–49, 65–83, 88

Daimyo, 23, 24
Daiwa Bank, 140
Daiwa Securities, xxiii, 35
Davidson, William, xxiii
Dazai, 26
Debt structure, 133–146, 151–165

Debt-to-equity, 141–145, 153–155, 160, 161
Declining industries, 8, 11, 62
Deficit, trade, 27, 97
  See also trade frictions
Denationalization, 7
Deregulation, industry, 7
Diet, Japanese, 6
Dividend payments, 143, 144, 153
DKB Group, 125
Duty, 5

East Germany, 49
Eastman Kodak Co., 120, 148
Economic Planning Agency, 10
Edo, 24
Eisai Pharmaceutical Co., 104
Electrical machinery industry, 36, 37, 144, 145, 161
Electronics industry, 37, 56, 62, 120, 126, 144, 145
Elite universities, 6, 18
Employment, lifetime, 27, 39–41, 52, 94, 95, 123
  private-sector, 6, 8, 13
  public-sector, 6, 9, 13, 18
  stability of, 90, 91, 95, 97, 116, 117, 119, 123
Eurocurrency market, 34, 155
Expatriates, 30, 39, 40, 44, 45
  See also host country nationals
Export development, 17, 92, 117
Export-Import Bank of Japan, 35, 89
Export-Import Law, 12
Export restraints, 18, 19, 87, 126
Export Trading Act, xxi, xxii
Export trading companies, xxii
  See also general trading companies
Exxon, 121, 148

Federal Trade Commission, 12
Federation of Economic Associations, 13
Feudal lord, 23
Financing function, 33–36, 44, 56, 75, 120
Financial structure, xxiii, xxiv, 11, 133–146, 151–165
Food and Drug Administration, 100, 101
Food industry, 38, 44, 66, 67, 75

INDEX

Ford Motor Co., 58
Foreign direct investment, xxi, 33, 37, 41–44, 59, 63, 102, 109–113, 146
Foreign exchange, 34, 35, 42, 68, 90, 155, 157
Foreign Exchange Bank Law, 139
Foreigners, attitude toward, xix, 27
Forest products, 44
Frutaful, 100
Fuji Heavy Industries, 88, 89
Fujisawa Pharmaceutical Co., 104, 106, 107, 111
Fujitsu Ltd., 123, 125, 149
Fuyo Group, 125

Gaigins, xix
General Agreement on Tariffs and Trade, xxi
General Electric Corp., 127, 147
General Electric Trading Corp., xxii
General trading companies, xx, xxi, 33–183, 142
Genetic engineering, xxii
Gensaki, 165
Glaxo, 107, 108
Gould Inc., 121, 147
Government-enterprise interface, xix, 3–30
Great Depression, 25
Green Cross Pharmaceutical Co., 104
Group consciousness, 30
Growth industries, 8, 11, 50, 58

Hans, 23, 24
Hajime, Nakamura, 25
Harvard University, xxi
Hayashi, Kichiro, xx, 33
Hitachi Ltd., 125
Hoechst, 105, 106, 108
Homogeneity of people, 5, 6, 30, 117, 121, 124
Honda Motor Co., 19, 117, 118
Host country nationals, xx, xxi, 30, 39–41, 43, 45, 52
Human resources, utilization of, xxiii, 115, 116
   See also staffing policies
Hungary, 49

IBM Corp., 50, 125, 147
IC Industries, 121

Import promotion, 10, 28, 92
Import restrictions, 17, 26, 27, 66
   See also nontariff barriers
Indonesia, 48
Industrial Bank of Japan, 35, 139
Industrial policy, xix, xxiii, 12, 14, 16–21, 26
Industrial rationalization, 17
Industrial revenue bonds, 158
Industrial targeting, 91–97
Information gathering, 19, 33, 38–41, 43, 44, 55, 62
International Monetary Fund, 7
Internationalization, pressure for, 8, 34, 35, 37, 44, 104
Inventory control, 144, 145
Isoda, Takuro, xxiii, xxiv

Japan Aircraft Development Corp., 88–90
Japan Airlines, 88
"Japan Inc.," 15, 16, 116
Japan National Railway, 9, 10
Japan Trade Center/JETRO, xix, 12, 28
Johnson & Johnson, 105, 108, 148
Joint ventures, xxiii, 30, 38, 39, 42, 50, 59, 70, 71, 89, 90, 107–113, 125, 126

Kanban system, 144
Kawasaki Heavy Industries Ltd., 88, 89, 149
Keidanren, 13
Kennecott Corp., 51
Kohiyama, Hiroshi, xx, xxi
Kokusai-ka, 8
Kopinski, Thaddeus, xxi, xxii, 65
Koseisho, 100–102
Kushimoto Oshima, 24
Kyorin, 111

Lease, 158, 159
Liberalization of trade, 7, 17, 18, 34, 35, 146
   See also protectionism
Licensing, xxiii, 88, 109–113
Lifson, Thomas, xxi, 55
Lilly, 105, 108
Liquidity issues, 65, 67, 75, 161–165

Loan low-cost, 11
  policy, 30, 119, 134-146, 151-165
London, 35
Long-term orientation, 117-119, 139
Long-term Credit Bank of Japan, 139
Long-term Credit Bank Law, 139

Machinery, 37, 56, 95
Manchuria, 25
Manufacturing companies, 13, 36-38, 42, 47, 48, 87-128, 152, 160-162
Matsushita Electrical, 149, 162
Maurer, Reed, 112
McGraw, Tug, 47
Meiji era, 6, 7, 13
Mercantile system, 25
Merck & Co., xxii, 108-114, 148
Merck Sharp & Dohme International, xxii, xxiv, 105-114
Mexico, 28, 29
Michigan, University of, xxiii
Middle East, 39
Mining/metals companies, 19, 36, 41, 58, 149
Ministry of Finance, 10, 11, 13, 18, 34, 35
Ministry of Foreign Affairs, 27
Ministry of Health, 13
Ministry of International Trade and Industry, xix, 11-13, 15, 17-19, 25, 26, 91, 92, 94
Mitsubishi Corp., xxi, xxiv, 48-52, 125, 142, 143
Mitsubishi Electric, 50
Mitsubishi Heavy Industries Ltd., 88, 89, 149
Mitsubishi International Corp., xx
Mitsubishi Trust and Banking Co., 140
Mitsui, 40, 142
Mitsui Trust & Banking Co., 140
Mobil Oil Co., 121, 148
Mongols, 4
Motorcycle industry, 19, 118

National emergency/survival, 7-9, 24
National Health Scheme (NHI), 101-103
National projects, 12, 17, 19
Nationalism, 4
Nationalization, 7, 10, 24
Natural resources, 7, 15, 29, 37, 44, 55

Negotiating function, 33, 42, 73
Neoconfucianism, 5
Nikko Securities, 35
Nippon Cargo Airlines, 88
Nippon Credit Bank, 139
Nippon Electric Co. (NEC), 125, 149
Nippon Telegraph & Telephone, 9, 10
Nippon Trust & Banking Co., 140
Nixon shock, 8
Nomura Securities, 35
Nontariff barriers to trade, xx, 26
Norandi, 89
Norin-Chukin Bank, 139
Northrop, 69

Ogallala Acquifier, 28
Oil crises, 8, 53, 151, 153, 160, 161
Okinawa Bank, 140
Ombudsman, 27
Organization for Economic Cooperation and Development, 7
Organizational structure, 42, 44, 45, 52, 62, 63, 68-73, 75, 76, 115, 123
Original equipment manufacturer, 50, 126, 127
Overseas Economic Cooperation Fund, 35

Pan Am, 16
Paris, 35
Patents, 100
Peace of Westphalia, 4
Perry, Commodore, 23, 24
Petrochemical industry, 142
Petroleum industry, 51, 60, 165
  See also oil crises
Petroleum Industry Act, 10
Pfizer, 105-108, 111, 148
Pharmaceutical industry, xxii, xxiii, 13, 37, 99-114
Philippines, 44
Physicians, 102, 111
Population, pressure of, 7, 28, 29
Product life cycle, 121
Product systems, xxi, 55-62
Profit center, 76-79, 81
Propa, see sales representatives
Protectionism, 12, 16, 24, 28, 92
  See also liberalization of trade, trade frictions
Pucik, Vladimir, xxiii, 115

INDEX

Raw materials, *see* natural resources
Rearmament, 9
Research and development, 11, 17, 18, 87, 92, 100–104, 107, 109–114, 120, 123–125
Research & Development Corporation of Japan, 50
Revitalization efforts, 16, 20
   See also industrial policy
Risk-bearing function, 33, 89
River Rouge Works, 58
Robock, Stefan, xx, 33
Roche, 105, 107, 108
Rockwell International, 66
Rockwell Trading Co., 69
Roosevelt, Franklin D., 25
Royalty payments, 110

Sales representatives, 103, 106, 107, 111
Sangyo gorika seisaku, 17
Sankyo, 104
Sato, Mitsuaki, xix, 15
Savings, 146
Scherring, 107, 108
Semantic differences, xix, 3
Shipbuilding, 95, 96
Shipping companies, 159
Shingikai, 14
Shionogi & Co., Ltd., 104, 106, 107, 111, 149
Shoko-Chukin Bank, 139
Silicon Valley, 40
SmithKline Beckman, 105, 108
Software, 49, 50
Sogo Shosha, *see* general trading companies
Sony Corporation, 117, 125, 149
South Korea, 39
Southern California, University of, xxiii
Southwest Airlines, 88
Sri Lanka, 39
Staffing policies, xx, xxi, 52
   See also expatriates, host country nationals
State trading organizations, 74
Steel industry, 11, 16, 34, 36, 38, 95, 96, 144
Streptomycin, 109
Stromberg-Carlson, 50
Subcontracting, 88, 89

Subsidies, granting of, 10, 11, 17, 103, 104
Sugar industry, 34, 36
Sumitomo Group, 125, 143
Sumitomo Metal Mining Co. Ltd., 19, 149
Supreme Court, 25
Swap transactions, 157
Swiss franc market, 155, 157
Switch transactions, 47, 49

Tagamet, 100
Taisho era, 24
Takeda, 104, 106, 107, 110, 111
Takeda-Abbott, 110
Tao Domestic Airlines, 88
Tax incentives, 18, 92, 120, 158, 159
Technology, development of, 11, 14, 47, 49, 62, 91–97, 114, 118
   See also research and development
Television industry, 126
Tendai Buddhism, 26, 38
Textile industry, 11, 16, 56–58, 125
Third country trade, 43, 48, 49
Third party trade, 79, 80
Tokugawa, 5, 23, 24
Tokyo University, 26
Toray, 125
Torii, 112
Toyo Trust & Banking Co., 140
Toyota Motor Co., 123, 149, 162
Trading associations, 14, 26
   See also Federation of Trade Associations
Trade frictions, 9, 16, 20, 21, 100–102
Trading function, 33
   See also general trading companies
Training programs, 41, 42, 52, 62
Transportation function, 33, 36–38, 65–83
Tung, Rosalie L., xvii
Twain, Mark, 53

United Airlines, 88
University of Texas at Dallas, xx

Van Zandt, George, 24
Van Zandt, Howard, xix, xx, 23
Van Zandt, Paul C., 24

Whirlpool, 125
Wimpfheimer, Leonard, xxii, 99
World War II, 6, 17, 25, 109, 139,
    142, 143

Yamaichi Securities, 35
Yamanouchi Pharmaceutical Co., 104,
    106
Yamaha Motors, 123
Yasuda, 142
Yasuda Trust & Banking Co., 140
Yoshino, Michael, 42

Zaibatsu, 8, 24, 142

ABOUT THE CONTRIBUTORS

Thomas J. Bacher is Director of International Business, Boeing Commercial Airplane Company. As director he is responsible for integrating Boeing's strategy and plans concerning international collaboration of new derivative programs and for determining appropriate response to offset requests as related to specific sales campaigns. In this capacity he interfaces with foreign industry/trade/economic ministries as well as aerospace companies of the countries involved in such business arrangements. In the course of such coordination, he has visited most of the aircraft companies throughout the world, including Japan, Europe, Australia, Canada, and China. In addition to some twelve years in the field of international business, his tenure with Boeing includes another twenty years of diverse experience in the company's commercial program divisions, military/aerospace divisions, and corporate headquarters. He has spoken at many conferences and seminars, including those sponsored by the London Financial Times, the American Management Association, the Industrial Conference Board, and several universities.

Robert J. Ballon is Professor of International Business and Labor Relations at Sophia University (Tokyo). He holds a doctorate "honoris causa" from the Catholic University of Cordoba (Argentina). Professor Ballon was born in Belgium and has lived in Japan since 1948.

His professional interest has concentrated upon Japanese labor-management relations and Japan's position in international business. He is founder and director of the International Management Development Seminars held at Sophia University since 1964. He is the editor/author of several books, including *Doing Business in Japan, Joint Ventures and Japan, The Japanese Employee, Foreign Investment and Japan, Marketing in Japan,* and *Financial Reporting in Japan,* and is a frequent contributor to international and Japanese professional journals. He serves as a consultant to numerous U.S. and European multinational corporations and is counsellor for Belgium's external trade (Japan).

William Davidson is Associate Professor of Management and Organization at the University of Southern California (USC). Prior to joining USC, he taught at the University of Virginia and Dartmouth College. Davidson holds an A.B. in Economics from Harvard College and an M.B.A. and D.B.A. from Harvard Business School. Dr. Davidson's work focuses on global industry and competition analysis, the management of technology, and corporate strategy formulation. His most recent book is *The Amazing Race: Winning the Technorivalry with Japan.* He has published articles on a variety of international management issues in journals such as *Harvard Business Review, Sloan Management Review,* the *Journal of International Business Studies,* and the *Journal of Business Research.* Dr. Davidson has served as a consultant to agencies of the U.S. and Canadian governments and to a number of companies in the information technology and other industries.

Kichiro Hayashi is Professor of International Management at the School of International Politics, Economics and Business, Aoyama Gakuin University in Tokyo. He received his Ph.D. and M.B.A. from Indiana University and his B.A. from Kobe University in Japan. He has taught at several North American universities, including UCLA and McMaster University, and was consultant for the United Nations CTC. Professor Hayashi's interests include international management, Japanese management, and strategic decisionmaking and planning. His numerous publications include articles in the *Academy of Management Journal* and *Management International Review.* His most recent book, *Cross-Cultural Interface Management,* was awarded the Prime Minister Ohira's Memorial Prize in 1985.

ABOUT THE CONTRIBUTORS 175

Takuro Isoda is President of Daiwa Securities (America) Inc. His previous positions with Daiwa included General Manager, Daiwa Europe N.V. and Daiwa Europe (Deutschland) GmbH (1980-1981); General Manager, Institutional Advisory Department and International Administration and Planning Department, Daiwa Securities Co. Ltd. (1981-1982); General Manager, International Brokerage Department, Daiwa Securities Co. Ltd. (1982-1984). In 1983 Mr. Isoda was elected to the Board of Directors, Daiwa Securities Co. Ltd., Tokyo.

Hiroshi Kohiyama is Director of Mitsubishi Corporation, Japan. He is a graduate of Tokyo University (1949) and joined Mitsubishi Corporation in 1955. His previous positions with Mitsubishi included President of Mitsubishi France (1972-1976); General Manager, Finance Division, Mitsubishi Corporation, Tokyo (1979-1982); and Executive Vice-President of Mitsubishi International Corporation, New York (1982-1984).

Thaddeus Kopinski is the Senior Editor of *Business International*. Since 1980 he has reported on all aspects of Washington policy, legislative and regulatory developments affecting international trade and investments for *Business International*, and other Business International publications. He worked for five years in Business International's East European Bureau in Vienna as an editor of *Business Eastern Europe*, covering Moscow and other East European capitals. Before joining Business International in 1975, Mr. Kopinski was a correspondent for UPI and the *London Financial Times* in Warsaw, Prague, and Bonn and a contributor to the *New York Times* and *Time* magazine. He is also the coauthor of monographs on technology transfer and joint ventures. Mr. Kopinski is the author and editor of Business International's Research Report, *Threats and Opportunities of Global Countertrade: Marketing, Financing, and Organizational Implications*. He is also the author of *Countertrade Options in Latin America*. Mr. Kopinski is a graduate of Cleveland State University. He holds an M.A. from Columbia University and a Social Sciences Certificate from the University of Warsaw. He has lectured on countertrade and Washington foreign trade issues at numerous seminars and conferences.

ABOUT THE CONTRIBUTORS

Thomas B. Lifson currently holds a research appointment at Harvard University's Center for International Affairs in the Program on U.S.-Japan Relations. He is also a Visiting Associate Professor of Economics at Columbia University's Faculty of International and Public Affairs. His doctoral degree is from The Harvard University Department of Sociology, and he has previously worked as an Assistant Professor at Harvard Business School. Dr. Lifson combines teaching and research in universities with management consulting to firms in both the United States and Japan. His major field of interest is the organization of business in Japan.

Vladimir Pucik is Assistant Professor of International Business and Organizational Behavior at the Graduate School of Business, the University of Michigan. He received his master's degree in international affairs—specializing in East Asia—and his Ph.D. in business administration from Columbia University. His research interest includes the linkage of competitive strategies with human resource management, issues in management in multinational firms, management of innovations, and comparative management with a particular emphasis on Japan. He has published extensively in academic and professional journals, such as the *Academy of Management Review, Columbia Journal of World Business, Human Resource Management, Organizational Dynamics*, and *Japan Economic Journal.* He consults to firms in the United States, Japan, and Europe.

Stefan H. Robock is Robert D. Calkins Professor Emeritus of International Business at the Graduate School of Business, Columbia University. Professor Robock received his M.A. and Ph.D. in Economics from Harvard University and joined the faculty of Columbia University in 1967 after serving as Director of International Business Studies at Indiana University from 1960 to 1967. Prior to beginning an academic career he worked as an economist for private and government agencies. He has undertaken overseas assignments for the United Nations; World Bank; Ford Foundation; and the U.S. government in India, Colombia, Bolivia, the Philippines, Bangladesh, Liberia, Malawi, and other countries. Professor Robock is the author of seven books and numerous articles in the fields of international business, inflation, economic development, and nuclear power, including one of the best-selling international business texts, *International Business* *and Multinational Enterprises* (Irwin, 1983), which is coauthored with Professor Kenneth Simmonds of the London Business School.

Mitsuaki Sato is President of Japan Trade Center (New York), the overseas arm of the Ministry of International Trade and Industry (MITI). Since joining MITI some twenty-six years ago, Mr. Sato has been actively involved in government policy formulation and decisionmaking in the fields of commerce and industry. He has lived in London for three years as a representative of JETRO. In addition, Mr. Sato has served as head of the Planning Division and the Planning and Coordination Department at JETRO headquarters. Mr. Sato is a graduate of Tokyo University (1958) and holds an M.A. in Economics from Columbia University.

Howard F. Van Zandt, Professor Emeritus, University of Texas at Dallas, has lived in Japan during three different periods for a total of twenty-seven years. His most recent assignment lasted seventeen years when he was in charge of ITT's interests there and in neighboring countries. He served as a director of two of Japan's largest manufacturing companies among many others. As President of the American Chamber of Commerce in Japan he learned of the problems encountered by other U.S. companies. He has given some 1,800 speeches about Japan, written over 500 articles and six books, and crossed the Pacific 128 times, many times on consulting assignments. Professor Van Zandt was bestowed the Order of the Rising Sun by the Japanese Emperor in June 1972.

Leonard Wimpfheimer is Director, Japan-China Operations, Merck Sharp Dohme International (MSDI). He holds a B.S. and M.S. degree from M.I.T. in Chemical Engineering and joined Merck in 1957 as a Process Engineer. He joined MSDI Japan Operations in 1980. His present responsibilities include Japanese administrative and business activities in corporate headquarters, as well as coordinating and supporting a broad range of business activities between the Japanese operating units and the corporate and divisional staffs to ensure optimization of Japanese business performance. He also maintains close contact with Japanese organizations and companies that have representative offices in the United States.

ABOUT THE EDITOR

Rosalie L. Tung is Professor of Business Administration and Director, International Business Center, University of Wisconsin, Milwaukee. She was invited as the first foreign expert to teach management at the Foreign Investment Commission—now known as the Ministry of Foreign Economic Relations and Trade—the highest agency under the Chinese State Council that approves all joint ventures and other major forms of foreign investment. Professor Tung is the author of five other books: *Management Practices in China, U.S.-China Trade Negotiations, Chinese Industrial Society after Mao, Business Negotiations with the Japanese*, and *Key to Japan's Economic Strength: Human Power.* She has also published widely on the subjects of international comparative management, international human resource management, international business negotiations, and organizational theory in leading international journals. Professor Tung served as Division Chairperson, International Management Division, Academy of Management (1984-1985) and is currently Treasurer and Member of the Executive Board, Academy of International Business. She has been appointed as a member of the Commercial Panel of Arbitrators, American Arbitration Association and is actively involved in management development and consulting activities around the world.